From Earth's Creation to John's Revelation

INTERFACES

Series Editor: Barbara Green, O.P.

From Earth's Creation
to John's Revelation

The INTERFACES Biblical Storyline Companion

Barbara Green, O.P.
Carleen Mandolfo
Catherine M. Murphy

A Michael Glazier Book

THE LITURGICAL PRESS

Collegeville, Minnesota

www.litpress.org

A Michael Glazier Book published by The Liturgical Press

Cover design by ●●●●●●●●●●●●●

1	2	3	4	5	6	7	8

Library of Congress Cataloging-in-Publication Data

Author

CONTENTS

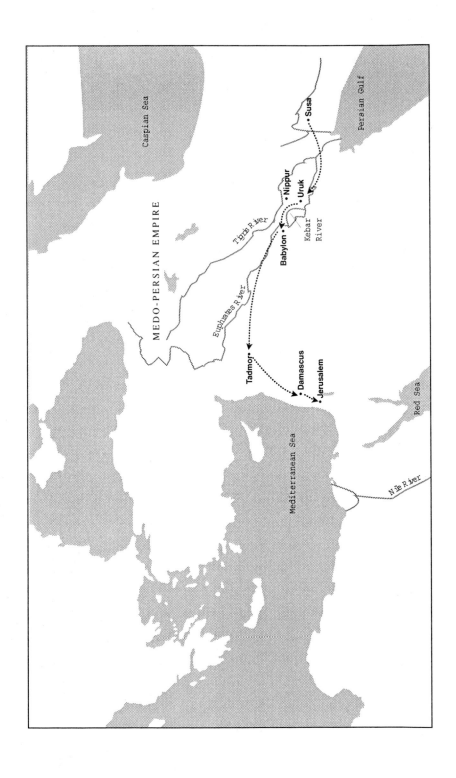

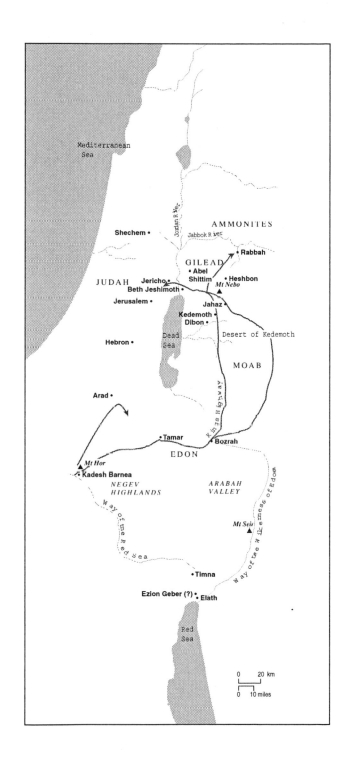

FROM EARTH'S CREATION
TO JOHN'S REVELATION

The INTERFACES Biblical Storyline Companion

Welcome!

The Bible starts, as you probably know, with two stories of origins, creation, beginnings. We will start there too and work our way through to the end, with the transformation of creation known via John of Patmos in the book of Revelation. We will go in order. What order, you ask? I could say it will be Bible order, except that our Bibles do not all go in the same order. It is, I hope, chronological order. But again, you might ask me if it is the order of events as they occurred, people as they lived, or an order set in some other way, by some writer working considerably later and scooping up old stories to reset for new occasions. These are good and important distinctions.

If you or someone else were writing your life story, the starting point might not be the day you were born! At the very least, it is probable that your life story will have become noteworthy for some reason that occurred much later than your arrival in the world. Mothers or fathers may start a baby book when their first child arrives; most of those books do not contain many filled pages. The Bible is different. It is not a series of journal entries made day by day as a writer runs alongside the biblical communities and records their doings. Nor is it primarily a book for children. Too many people enjoy it as children, reject it when they become appropriately critical in adolescence, and never return to it. But that is another story. The goal of this book is to help you turn or return to the Bible as an adult, aware as you are now of the complexities of human communication and relationship.

This particular account will follow biblical story order, by which I mean the long story line stretching from Adam and Eve to the Christian community of John the seer. For a good part of the way that storyline is not

1

difficult to pick out. We will leave for later, you and I and the various authors of our INTERFACES books, to sort out the questions of when and how the stories were produced and used—and most importantly, by whom. But so that we have a rough idea, count on the fact that the biblical text as we know it today began to take shape sometime around the middle of the first millennium B.C.E. (Before the Common Era—perhaps in the 600s or 500s, though undoubtedly drawing from much older material), in the way that a patchwork quilt might be made of older scraps of clothing but sewn together for some later occasion. The process seems likely to have been completed around the end of the first century of the Common Era. We will also reserve for the moment the questions of revelation and inspiration that often attend discussion of the Bible. It will be enough here to provide a coherent narrative from the Bible of the dealings of God and the Hebraic/Jewish and Christian communities. Though your Bible may seem heavy when you carry it around, it is amazingly compact for the amount of recital it offers us.

Origins Stories (Set pre-1000 C.E.)

1. Adam and Eve

Since we are focusing on biblical characters, it is appropriate to call this first scene Adam and Eve. You will appreciate that it could also have been called creation. The Bible's first book, Genesis, starts us with two stories of the origins of all that the ancients knew from their observation of things. The first runs from Genesis 1:1–2:4. It is famously set up in terms of days of the week: six days of creation and a seventh for God's rest. Readers love this first story for its orderliness. You might imagine it as a huge old roll-top desk built with many cubbyholes and drawers. Order reigns by a number of criteria. After the challenge of starting the story from some point of pre-creation difficult to imagine, the storyteller shows us God, apparently alone but speaking in the plural, ordering or inviting into existence light and darkness, the cosmos, the earth, day, and the many waters. The animals—some named and others implied—make their way in their environments of water, air, and land, all in their proper places. Though humans may consider themselves to be the crown of creation, it is as true that they come last onto the scene. But arrive they do, simultaneously, a man and a woman, both made in the image and likeness of God and given a commission by God. They are given a position of responsibility and urged to multiply (as are the land animals; the plants do not need to be told). The humans make no response here; but keep reading! As God creates, we also hear a continual reflective appraisal: Everything is good. Perhaps the crown of creation is God's pleasure in it all, and God's resting to savor all that is.

If one story of creation is good, two are better. So Genesis 2:4–3:24 gives us another one. If the first story is characterized by careful and almost fussy orderliness, the second seems constructed quite differently. It also stumbles a bit over the difficulty of pushing off from what is unknown but then shows God not so much issuing orders or invitations as hunched over a moistened clay artifact, shaping it into some semblance of a human being. Once that earthy creature has taken shape, God plants it in a garden, a place that perhaps contains the same representatives of the universe we met previously, but without the first story's detail. Attention focuses first on two trees and then on one animal. This story shows the proto-human giving way to a pair, a man and a woman. We spend little time with them before their choices (the woman's first and the man's second) change the scene dramatically. The life of caring for and tending the garden, of eating its produce, and evidently of enjoying intimacy with God comes to an end once the couple eats the fruit that had been withheld from them by divine decree. You will notice that though the story seems not to approve their choice—or at least seems to indicate that in its wake came various breaches of solidarity between the humans, between them and God, between them and the animals—there is no mention of sin or inherited guilt or wrong. The outcome of their choice is that the woman and man exit the garden and take up residence in the world as we know it. By the end of the story they have their names: Adam and Eve. The Jewish community calculates that date to have been (at the recent millennium) 5760 years ago.

If two stories of creation are good, more are better yet! And so the topic of creation is mentioned in many other places: at the end of Job, in certain psalms (e.g., Psalm 105), in the writings of the poet we will later call Second Isaiah, in the beginning of the Gospel of John, in certain hymns of Paul (who will add some of the familiar overtones of inherited guilt to the story of Adam and Eve). And creation is implied in many other places, often as waters roil and new deeds are done. Another place to find stories of creation is Wisdom writings (e.g., Proverbs 8, Wisdom of Solomon). There you will find the figure of Sophia (or Wisdom), an attendant at creation, helping the first couple, at play before God. Let me introduce myself: I am Sophia, divine Wisdom, asked to be your guide here, since I was there from the start and have always been a presence since creation. Welcome!

2. Noah, Family and Friends

Once the first man and woman leave the garden of Eden their struggles become a bit more familiar to most human beings. Though the whole narrative of the eating of forbidden fruit is a powerful symbol for the human condition of interdependence and its breach—humans with each other, with all of the rest of creation, and with God—the next moral deed described is when Adam and Eve's firstborn, Cain, kills his brother Abel in a deed that looks like jealousy (told in Genesis 4). Some readers, in fact, stress that the sin of fratricide looks more classic to the human species than does the more complex and subtle transgression of the first man and woman. In any case, as Genesis continues its narrative of the ancestors of all human beings (there are several genealogical listings in these early chapters of Genesis), isolated and self-seeking sinfulness is a prominent motif. God registers regret over the fact that evil has taken over substantially and moves to change the ways of creation. Though you may be more accustomed to language that stresses that God is all-powerful and all-knowing, that is not the impression most careful readers take away from these old Hebrew Bible stories. Selecting a rare good man to survive with his family, God directs him to get ready for a huge flood so that at least a pair of every creature can be saved and all can start afresh. The building of the ark is carefully overseen by God, and its architecture is reminiscent of later important worship sites. The actual gathering of the animals is not described, though directions are given, and it is of course deeply symbolic rather than meant to be literal. Many cultures have flood stories (and the Bible itself more than one), since they open such wonderful possibilities of rebirth, fresh starts, cleansings, and so forth. The destruction of life as the floodwaters rise is the poignant side of the story, making clear the seriousness of the situation God is seeking to address. My role in the story, at least as told later in Wisdom of Solomon, is to help Noah steer the ark through dangerous waters.

When it is safe for Noah, his wife, sons, and daughters-in-law and all the pairs of animals to leave the ark after many days of floating and waiting, they do so. Noah offers a sacrifice to God, with feelings not described but easy to imagine. God, smelling the savor of the sacrifice, has strong feelings too, the storyteller reports, and vows not to flood the earth again. Whether because of the good odors or for some other reason related to divine experience, God establishes new procedures for how human beings will eat. Prior to the flood the human community had been vegetarian. After the flood they are given a permission or concession to eat animals, provided that the blood is carefully drained as the animal is slaughtered. As the flood story ends, Noah apparently experiments with liquid refreshments as well and drinks too much wine, an episode that leads to some sort of unfilial behavior on the part of the youngest son Ham, who is cursed for it. As the communities of the earth take up their post-flood lives it becomes clear that a fresh start does not solve the problem of human sinfulness. The stories and the interweaving genealogies and verbal maps seem to be later

Israel's effort to account for the neighborhood as it was known at the time of writing. Like all people telling their own origins story, Israel maps from the center, putting itself at the eye of the world.

3. Abraham and Sarah, Isaac and Rebekah

The story of the Jewish people starts officially with the first parents, called from outside the land where they would be invited to live, brought from a Mesopotamian civilization of the ancient Near East (perhaps to be understood as early Babylon). Though there are some sixteen chapters of Genesis stories about them (Genesis 12–27) and their offspring—son Isaac and cousin Rebekah, whom Isaac marries—the stories all show how God and these early forebears consistently struggle to work out viable relationships. Covenant is one name for it, but like any relationship it comes down to a matter of care, trust, and communication. God's communication with Abraham and Sarah takes a variety of forms—visions, voices, angelic visitors, and silence—and the subjects discussed are most often that they would be given the land (called Canaan), would have many descendants, and would stand in a relationship of blessing to others outside the family. That sounds good, but for Abraham and Sarah it is not so easy. Both of them are by this time old, and they have no child from their marriage. As everyone must do who is communicating with God and seeking an active relationship, they attempt various ways to enact what God has promised: in this case, to have a child. One of their efforts, collaborating with Sarah's Egyptian maid Hagar (or using her), produces Ishmael, ancestor of the Arab peoples. But only in God's own good time and in the traditional way of human beings is Isaac conceived, heir of the promises made to his parents. Even once he is on the scene, the ancestors' struggles continue in fresh editions. The most mysterious, most revered, and possibly most frightening of the stories told is about how Abraham comes close to sacrificing his son on a mountain, restrained only at the last minute by God. There is no plumbing the depths of this story, no way of resolving the mystery of the communication between God and Abraham that seems to shut out Sarah and even Isaac himself. My role was to steady Abraham to do what he was told to do and to console and confide in them all as they pore over the memories left by that event.

So far as land is concerned, that promise remains mostly ahead of them as well. Though Abraham and Sarah traverse the land of Canaan and build altars from time to time, even prosper there, they are also forced out and off the land by famine on occasion, and have adventures of one sort or another with the indigenous dwellers (called by various names, most famously Canaanites and Philistines). The only land Abraham can actually claim is the plot he purchases to bury his dead, the family tomb at Hebron, which is revered—and contested—to this day. No less mysterious to the family than God's commitment to them for land and progeny is the indication that they are to be a blessing to others. Though occasionally there are moments of blessing, more often you hear of disputes with others over land or words, over hospitality or disputed rights. Abraham may not have felt like a blessing, and his peers might have agreed with him. The teller of these varied and perhaps motley stories of the first Jewish people continues to explain how various of the later neighbors came to populate the region. When Sarah dies, Abraham marries again and begets more children. But Isaac is the son through whom the line is to go, and so he is provided with not a local woman to marry but one of the kin from Mesopotamia, Rebekah, niece of Abraham, who bears the twins Esau and Jacob. But before we go ahead to that part of the story, a quick reflection about Abraham and Sarah.

You might think that, being the primary ancestors, they would feature prominently in the narratives ahead. In fact, they do not. Their names appear from time to time—his more than hers, as you would expect. Abraham comes to epitomize or stand for various things. He is made, especially in the New Testament, a paradigm of faith. That is true in a certain sense, so long as you understand that part of what he stands for is the struggle to believe in what God promised but had not quite followed through on in detail. To be promised a child in old age sounds easy, but another way to think about the story is that, except for the very occasional and succinct word from God during the decades between their call to move to Canaan and the appearance of Isaac, it is not at all clear to them in detail what they need to do. Their faith, not unlike that of their much later descendants, must not be mistaken for easy certainty. Like all who try to understand how God communicates, Abraham and Sarah feel their way along mostly in the dark and in mystery. Abraham also becomes paradigmatic for being the ancestor of Gentiles as well as Jews, a theme that comes up for us intermittently when such issues press, notably around the time of the return from exile in Babylon (the sixth or fifth century). Paul, much later, also uses events from the life of Abraham and Sarah contrastively, to make clear certain points about how God deals. The foundational stories are rich and open to many appropriations, part of the gift of Scripture. But stay rooted in these Genesis stories themselves that describe, or at least suggest, that the wonderful challenge of doing what these human beings think God wished them to do is never easy for these early ancestors. Now back to Isaac, Rebekah, and their twin boys.

4. *Jacob and Family*

Introducing Jacob to you is a bit tricky. He's a complex man, probably one of the most complex and intriguing characters to move through the pages of the Bible. Although some of the figures you have met (and will meet) might have seemed a bit one-dimensional, at least compared to folks you read about in modern literature, the same cannot be said of Jacob. Just some of the adjectives used to describe Jacob might include: conniving, clever, ruthless, devoted, selfish, wise, immature. If I had to sum him up in a word, I'd have to say Jacob is a "survivor," an attribute I take some credit for; I am his constant companion and guide (Wisdom 10). As a reliable judge of the moral sagacity of a person, I must admit I would probably not hold up Jacob as a role model, but what can be said is that he is quintessentially human, a character most people can relate to.

Jacob is one of twin sons born to Isaac and Rebekah, and even the early details of his birth hint at the man Jacob becomes. Before Rebekah gives birth she receives a message from God that prophesies the destinies of her two sons (Genesis 25). She is told that as the two are struggling in her womb (she is having a rough pregnancy), so will they struggle in life, but the younger will supersede the elder (thus challenging the ancient Near Eastern custom of primogeniture). Tension between brothers, often predicated on the issue of patrimony, is not uncommon in biblical stories (recall Cain and Abel, Ishmael and Isaac). Indeed, when Rebekah finally gives birth we are told that Jacob enters the world holding onto the heel of his older brother, Esau—a foreshadowing of the reversal of fortune previously prophesied? Or is he merely hitching a ride down the birth canal? We aren't told, but as the story unfolds this symbolic moment becomes clearer.

While he is still young Jacob is described as something of a "mama's boy"; he enjoys staying in the tents with Rebekah, while his brother, Esau, is described as "hairy" and a youth who enjoys hunting and the outdoors. Subsequent to their birth, the first instance in which we see the brothers interact reveals Jacob working hard to turn the prophecy his mother received into a reality. Esau comes in from the fields famished, near to death if we're to believe his self-assessment, and Jacob bargains for his older brother's birthright in exchange for some stew (Genesis 25). As the next scene unfolds we discover that Jacob isn't satisfied with obtaining only Esau's birthright, and, on Jacob's behalf, it seems Rebekah is not satisfied, either. She sends Jacob, in the guise of his brother, to the dying Isaac. Isaac is duped into bestowing on Jacob the blessing traditionally reserved for the elder. When Esau discovers the ruse he is overcome, and begs his father for a blessing. But in the biblical world once solemn words are spoken they cannot be taken back, so Isaac is forced to give Esau a lesser blessing than he is entitled to by custom. Rebekah, fearing for Jacob's life, arranges to send him away to her relatives in Haran so that he might be safe, and so that he might find a wife among them (Genesis 27).

As Jacob sets out on his journey, God's presence is made known to him as the god of his grandfather, Abraham, and his father, Isaac. God repeats to Jacob the covenantal promises made to Abraham and Isaac, promises of land, children, and security. Interesting, though easy to overlook, is the conditional nature of Jacob's response to God's unconditional promise: Jacob replies that *if* God will do these things, and bring him home safely, *then* YHWH will be his god (Genesis 28).

Upon arriving in Haran, Jacob is warmly welcomed into is mother's brother's household by his uncle, Laban. But as it turns out, Jacob's history of rocky interpersonal relations comes back to haunt him. Jacob falls in love with Laban's daughter Rachel, and asks Laban for her hand in marriage. Laban agrees, under the condition that Jacob commit to working for Laban for seven years as payment for Rachel. When the seven years are up, Jacob claims his bride, but in a moment of exquisite irony, after the ceremony, when Jacob has consummated the marriage, he discovers that Laban has duped him, and that he has married Rachel's older sister, Leah (Genesis 29). Jacob must work another seven years to secure the wife of his choice. Because she is less loved, God blesses Leah with six sons and a daughter, while Rachel, following in the footsteps of the matriarchs before her, has a difficult time conceiving. But she eventually does so, and gives birth to Joseph, whom Jacob (not surprisingly) favors over his older sons, and who thus, many years later, ends up being a flashpoint for family tragedy.

After amassing a fortune, largely at Laban's expense, Jacob flees from Laban with his two wives and several children (as well as Laban's household gods) to return to Canaan, his homeland (Genesis 31). In the course of his journey Jacob learns, to his dismay, that his brother Esau is on his way to meet him with a large number of men. The night before they are to meet, Jacob falls asleep on the bank of the Jabbok River, and during the night (while he is dreaming?) he wrestles with a "man" who blesses him and changes his name to "Israel" (which means "one who strives with God"), because according to the "man" Jacob has wrestled "with humans and with God and has prevailed." Jacob interprets the event as an encounter with God (Genesis 33). The next morning Jacob limps across the river, and with much fear and trembling confronts his brother. Contrary to Jacob's expectations, Esau embraces him and weeps, and the brothers are reconciled.

The wrestling match and subsequent crossing of the river serve as something of a metaphor for the new life that Jacob then embarks on. With nothing more to fear from his brother, Jacob settles in Bethel and makes good on the vow he made to God when he first set out from Canaan. He removes from his household all the idols his family has accumulated and sets up an altar to the God of his fathers. God reiterates the covenantal promise made earlier to Jacob and "officially" changes his name to Israel (Genesis 35). Rachel dies giving birth to a second son, Benjamin, and Esau and Jacob bury their father (hmm, wasn't he dying a long time ago?). Jacob's life has come full circle and the focus of the story now shifts to his sons, who sadly, though probably inevitably, carry on the familial turmoil set in motion by their father.

5. *Joseph and Family*

My care for the ancestors continues, whether or not that is always apparent to them, or to you, as you read. Jacob and his four wives produce twelve sons and one daughter. The daughter, Dinah, shifts away from the main family when she marries into a Canaanite family (Genesis 34) after a complex episode involving violence of several types. The rest of the "Jacob family" does not prosper very happily without the active intervention of the women, who have faded from the story, though of course not from life. Favoritism and factions split the men. Joseph, son of Rachel, is favored by his father and given a singular coat: many colors, long sleeves, in any case not very practical for work. His position in regard to the others is both reflected in and refracted by a pair of dreams he has and shares, dreams that the others—his brothers and father—interpret to their own disadvantage. Thinking that the dreams signal his sense of superiority above the rest of them, both his father Jacob and Joseph's ten half-brothers seem determined to put him down in several ways, some quite literal. One day when Jacob, foolishly perhaps, sends his favorite to check on the others who are shepherding the family flocks, his brothers seize Joseph and put him down a well. Confusion ensues. The ten brothers rehearse a number of plans for being rid of Joseph, and somehow in the confusion he is vanished, sold down to Egypt without anyone quite understanding completely how events had transpired (Genesis 37). But Joseph is safe in Egypt, and his brothers think they have indeed seen the last of him, once they get past the awkwardness and guilt of returning the blood-spattered coat to a grieving Jacob, whose demeanor and garb continue to testify that Joseph maintains a place no other will ever fill.

I remain with Joseph in Egypt—and with the others as well, though they rarely register or evidence it. I save Joseph and various of his companions from a series of dangers and help him with dream interpretation when he finds himself imprisoned in a pit again, thanks to an episode where his position of favor once more disturbs a household. Joseph gains a reputation for skill at dream interpretation, and finally on the day the Big Man of Egypt needs *his* dreams read, Joseph is summoned from an Egyptian jail. Pharaoh's dreams, like Joseph's, are a part of my care for the ancestors, since they presage world famine such that, after some years of plenty and storing, crops will fail and storehouses will begin to be depleted, drawing everyone to the land of the Nile, where Joseph's power, position, skill, and help from me will mean enough food has been gathered to sell. And so it goes. The sons of Jacob, brothers of Joseph, come shopping, and though they do not recognize the man who meets them at the storehouses, he knows them for his brothers, or at least ten of them. Now you will argue, and rightly so, about how Joseph's plan takes shape as he realizes his position of advantage over them: Does he recognize the "relative position motif" from his dreams of Genesis 37? Whether Joseph connects his own dreams as his ten brothers bow before him is up to you to decide. Of course the ten visitors are not thinking of the dreams, which are actually continuing to move as powerfully as ever. But whether you see Joseph's next moves as retaliating against his brothers, putting them through the same "ups and downs" through which they put him—down into a well, up and out, down into Egypt—or whether he seems to be scripting a path of reconciliation for them, the effect is the same. Joseph quizzes them about their family details, ascertains that there remains an old father and a youngest brother still at home, and insists that, should they wish more food (which he knows has to be the case), the youngest brother will need to accompany them on the next trip down.

Jacob is not happy about that stipulation, having already lost both Joseph and Simeon (the latter kept as hostage from the brothers' first shopping trip). But Jacob is nothing if not practical, so he gives in and allows Benjamin, full brother of Joseph, to accompany his brothers to Egypt to get more food. Joseph's machinations grow more complex and devious, and lest the brothers slip out of his presence again, even for another year, Joseph contrives a "sting," so that Benjamin is accused of—looks quite guilty of—stealing Joseph's valuable silver divining cup. So the brothers, who had hoped to be safely on their way with fresh supplies, are in worse trouble than before. As the story unfolds it is not so clear exactly what Joseph has in mind: likely some way to keep his youngest brother in his presence. But Judah, on whom I had also been working, rises beautifully to the occasion and begs to replace his "guilty" brother Benjamin as a prisoner, putting into the middle of the table with the rest of the bargaining devices the frailty and vulnerability of the wily old Jacob. If Benjamin does not come back,

Judah pleads shrewdly, the old man will die from grief. Stymied, and nudged by me, Joseph makes himself known to his brothers, who, it must be admitted, are more startled than pleased. But Joseph now gives voice to my ongoing insistence that the family all come down to Egypt. Joseph has it substantially right. The dreams, the fraternal joustings, all those things have happened in order to draw the family off the land and into safety. From what, you will ask, and that is difficult to explain. Their exile was necessary; diaspora (a later name for Jews living outside the land of promise) is not wholly bad, though it seemed so at the time. They just needed to go, and that is what they finally do. When Jacob and Joseph are reunited, the weeping resounds all the way to Pharaoh's palace. The whole group, grown now to seventy plus, resettles in the land of Egypt and prospers there (for a while). When Jacob dies they take him back to Hebron for burial but return again to Egypt themselves. Though every now and again his ten brothers worry that Joseph would retaliate in some way, I think that was never likely. He understands as well as is possible that what the brothers had done—in fact, what he had done, too—has become part of a larger and more mysterious plan. He was right, his perception helpful. And so the ancestral group, transplanted for the moment off the land of promise, thrives in Egypt, at least for a time (the whole story runs from Genesis 37–50).

6. Moses of the Egypt Experience

So far as Scripture is concerned, Moses is the most prominent Old Testament/Hebrew Bible figure. Though both his persona and the pattern of the exodus event (with which he is signally associated) recur in many parts of both testaments, his presence and story root massively in the books of Exodus, Leviticus, Numbers, and Deuteronomy. His own life has a dramatic beginning. After the family of Jacob settles in Egypt, thanks to Joseph and my Providential care, there appears to be a pause, where the link between YHWH and the ancient ancestors seems to weaken. A subsequent Pharaoh who "knows not Joseph" threatens the lives of Hebrew baby boys, and only thanks to the courageous resourcefulness of midwives (and mothers, of course) do some males manage to be born. Among them is the young Moses, who though saved at birth is entrusted to the Nile when it becomes too dangerous to keep him hidden. He is spotted by Pharaoh's daughter, who, with some behind-the-scenes help from Moses' sister Miriam, has him nursed by his own mother (Jochebed) until such time as he is brought to Pharaoh's palace to be raised there, apparently as an Egyptian. Partisan intervention on his part—first when he steps between a quarreling Egyptian-Hebrew pair and then when he interposes lethally between two Hebrews—necessitates his quick departure. The young Moses flees to the land of Midian, where he takes up the quiet life of a shepherd. In the meantime his people (his ostensible foster kin) have been reduced to harsh labor to build Egyptian cities. The piling up of misery finally becomes so heavy that the people cry out to YHWH, who, alert for such a plea, hears them and begins more visibly to respond (Exodus 1–2).

On what must have begun as a normal day for Moses he encounters the vitality and fidelity of God in a strange vision of a bush burning but not consumed, becomes the recipient of the particular name of God (YHWH), and is given a commission to go back to help his people. He is also promised the assistance of his brother Aaron as well as of God. Though Moses at first resists this appointment, going several rounds of debate over it with God, he finally returns to Egypt to begin his lifework of intermediation, moderating sides. The representation of the plight of the enslaved Hebrews, who often though not always want relief from their burdens, is in conflict with Pharaoh's felt need for cheap and handy labor. God's ultimate plans seem often at angles to what the human beings can see! Moses manages to alienate both sides, not so rare for an intermediary. The Hebrew slaves blame him when his intervention seems simply to draw more attention to them and increase their burdens. And the tendency of Pharaoh to toy with Moses, or in any case to renege on agreements made, results in a series of faceoffs between these powerful yet thwarted bargainers. On no less than ten occasions Moses seeks and seems to secure concessions from Pharaoh that are later either denied outright or are promised and then canceled summarily. There are many patterns to ponder in these stories of the plagues, as they are called, the consequences God and Moses effect when Pharaoh (with his famously hard heart) repeatedly refuses any relief for the enslaved. The land where the Hebrews live is not affected by the water-turned blood or by the several plagues of fearsome frogs, lots of locusts, irritating insects, and dread diseases, or by the wicked weather phenomena of hail, thunder, or thick darkness. But the Egyptians suffer increasingly, as does their land, as the episodes follow upon each of Pharaoh's waffling negotiations. Finally Moses, and surely God, have had enough.

The narrative shifts to tell of the ritual preparations for the primordial and paradigmatic event of liberation, how the people are instructed to prepare what is narrated as the first Passover. On the night of its celebration God strikes the firstborn of all Egyptian male living beings, and Pharaoh's desperation is such that he gives the order to eject the "troublesome Hebrews" from the land. Moses and all the descendants of Abraham and Sarah—and miscellaneous others with them—start their journey of liberation suddenly, carrying unleavened bread in their shawls as they make their way hastily and not completely happily to the shores of the Red Sea. They are fearful, with some cause, since Pharaoh once again changes his mind, unable to recall or imagine himself losing his storecity builders. He sends his army after the Hebrews, massed now nervously at the water. Moses urges steadfastness and silence, reminds his people that God will see them through the water, and indeed, so it happens. God orders Moses to extend his rod over the waters, which part, allowing access for the fleeing Hebrews but closing up on the pursuing Egyptians. The slaves cross, the oppressors sink, and Moses' sister Miriam leads the community in song and dance to make the event memorable, ritualized, and an act of worship. The Jewish celebration of Passover to this day memorializes in prayer those Egyptians who lost their lives and often other—even contemporary—opponents of the Jewish people as well. It seems, perhaps, that the community can return home to Canaan in a short time, since a quick look at the map will remind you of how short the distance is. But Moses, with an intuition of the people's weaknesses, decides that they need more time and formation in the wilderness, so the narrative takes characters and readers south instead of north.

7. Moses between Egypt and Canaan

Moses and the Israelites are not the first (or the last) to suppose that once they were out of a crisis their troubles are nearly over. In fact, as Moses reviews the rest of the story with the people just before he leaves them for the last time (in Deuteronomy), his recounting of the whole story of just how the community has arrived at the east bank of the Jordan River focuses primarily on the story of what happened *after* the Red Sea was crossed. In the biblical books (from Exodus 16 to its end, in all of Leviticus, Numbers, and Deuteronomy) the storyline often seems somewhat obscured by long sections of legal material that almost overwhelm it. Still, I think you can find your way neatly enough through the complicated story of these events, and perhaps even appreciate the Wisdom behind the superficially messy blending of story and legislation.

The short of it is that it takes forty years to get from Egypt to Canaan. The first part of the journey (to Mount Sinai, also called Horeb) and the very last part (from Kadesh to Moab) are relatively brief jaunts. The long part—some thirty-eight years—is spent wandering in between those spatial and temporal edges. But I am getting ahead of myself. When the community first emerges from Egypt and heads south there comes a series of episodes (related in Exodus 16–18 and also in Wisdom 11–19, where my role is made manifest) in which the people complain, murmur, and put God and Moses to the test. The ostensible issues are understandable enough:

struggles over food, water, and desert opponents. But underlying the complaints about too much or too little of those items sounds a repudiation of the whole process of liberation. These complaint episodes, in which both God and Israel often sound petulant and querulous, are actually serious engagements about whether Israel trusts God to go ahead with the process or not—and also whether God trusts Israel enough to form a serious relationship or not. In each event, when the people complain, God gives them something (manna, sweet water, military help, a better organizational structure). But the undertow of the whole set (which continues throughout the desert phase of the relationship between God and Israel) runs negative. A relationship is being forged, but not easily. The most important part of the whole forty years comes just (!) three months into the adventure: the giving of the law at Sinai/Horeb.

This huge set of material intervenes at Exodus 19 and runs pretty much until Numbers 11 (and dominates Deuteronomy as well). The essence of it is that God summons the community to receive and accept formally the particulars of the way in which Israel is to live and worship. The several accounts of this covenant, as it is often called in shorthand, stress ritually the importance of the encounter that sets for all time the general expectations between God and people (particulars always require existential negotiation). Though it is evident that, for the Hebrew (and Jewish) people as for others, law develops gradually and contextually, the Bible places virtually all of it at Sinai/Horeb to make clear its status as primordial and permanent. The mountain scene is formal, dramatic, perhaps frightening, surely memorable. The community, arranged hierarchically, encounters God. Moses' experience is particular since he remains on the mountain for forty days to get the whole set of material after the famous ten commandments have been communicated verbally to all assembled. Interestingly enough, and hardly coincidentally, while Moses and God are so engaged, the people commit for the first time (narrated-to-you) the sin named idolatry, which attempts in one way or another to corner and control God. The famous golden calf episode (Exodus 32–34 and Deuteronomy 5, 9, and 10) marks the signal temptation of the "new" community to misrepresent God in some way. It is the cardinal struggle between God and people, and an interesting one to plumb. But on this first occasion of it Aaron helps the people make the calf from their own gold jewelry, and God hears the worship noise and tells Moses. It is a risky moment, where God seems ready to trade in the exodus group and start again, but Moses intervenes to save the people—and God. God and Moses rework the law tablets (the first set is broken amid the melée of the calf event) and the story stops to detail portions of law, including the worship apparatus of the Sanctuary and the Ark of the Covenant. By the time the community reorganizes to leave the mountain they proceed ceremonially, ranked in order to signal their new status as God's specially chosen people. The whole adventure might have ended successfully soon after Sinai, since God signals a readiness to give the land of Canaan to the people right away. But they fear to take it, and after another counterproductive clash of wills God turns the people back toward the southwest, where they wander until the adults of the exodus generation die out. There is a series of episodes marking that long stretch of time, mostly unhappy, where the people continue to contend and fall into various versions of infidelity toward God, contest Moses' leadership, and the like. The wilderness period is occasionally valorized later (e.g., Hosea seems to speak well of it, and perhaps Ezekiel), but as recited in these four books it is a difficult if formative phase. My role in that long sojourn is to work with the people so that they can discern God's care for them somewhat against the grain of their experience and also against the backdrop of what happens to their several opponents. Or so the tradition develops as it is retold lavishly in Wisdom of Solomon in a later and just as dangerous time. But that is another story. Keep reading!

The wandering phase comes to a finish as God invites the people to leave Kadesh, to proceed carefully up through the territory of Edom and Moab, to fight and defeat two kings of the Amorites, and then to get ready to enter the land. The short version of all of this is the book of Deuteronomy, where Moses reprises for the community all "they" have been through, giving them once again a series of opportunities to consider their options, be conscious of their status with God, and appropriate the gift of relationship (including law and land) being offered. As Moses tells the story he wanders narratively himself, as if in imitation of the tale he is telling, and you will want to review his sense of how he suspects things are going to proceed in his absence. Oh yes, from the end of Deuteronomy on, Moses is (mysteriously) gone, replaced now by Joshua.

(Re-)Settlement in the Land (Set pre-1000 B.C.E.)

8. Joshua

Joshua represents the first generation after Moses to whom knowledge of me, Sophia, has been given as a gift from the LORD: I am revealed in *Torah,* given to Moses and the people on Mount Sinai (also called Mount Horeb), and Joshua, Moses' successor, is expected to pick up the baton and nurture the relationship between me and the people, Israel, now that Moses is dead (Deuteronomy 34).

God commissions (Deuteronomy 31) and Moses lays hands on (Deuteronomy 34) Joshua, demonstrating to him and all the people that Joshua is indeed Moses's legitimate successor, and now God's right-hand man. Joshua is enjoined to settle the people in the "promised land," a land promised some generations earlier to Abraham, Isaac, and Jacob. Concisely summarizing the physical and moral attributes that will be required to fulfill this task, God says to Joshua: "Only be strong and very courageous, being careful to act in accordance with all the law that my servant Moses commanded you . . ." (Josh 1:7). Joshua indeed needs to be brave and obedient to God's *torah*/instruction so as not to rouse God's anger against him or the people, and to succeed in his mission because, you see, the "promised" land is now also called home by a group of people called Canaanites, and it seems there cannot be enough room for everybody. More significantly, to keep me close in their hearts God requires the Israelites to remove completely any temptation to live according to the precepts of the gods worshiped by the Canaanites, ways of living that God considers abominable. As Moses had warned, if Israel fails to resist the lure of other gods YHWH will remove the people from the land. Such a dire consequence requires a firm, even harsh determination on the part of Israel to utterly destroy (an element of Israelite warfare called "the ban") the "dangerous others" already in the land.

Accordingly, in a reenactment of the Exodus crossing, Joshua leads the Israelites across a miraculously drying Jordan River into the land of Canaan. The first thing Joshua does is to reconsecrate the people to YHWH by circumcising all the men born during the wandering in the desert who thus had not yet had the sign of the covenant engraved on their flesh (Joshua 5). This marks a new beginning in the covenantal relationship between YHWH and the people. They then celebrate their first Passover in the new land and prepare to face their first battle, at Jericho. They had previously spied out the city with the help of a prostitute who lived there named Rahab, but it seems such preparation is unnecessary since this battle is clearly in YHWH's hands. A very ritualized procedure carried out by the Israelites follows, prescribed in great detail by God, involving trumpet blowing, ark carrying, circling, and shouting. The walls of Jericho simply fall down without a shot being fired, so to speak: a quintessential "holy war," and an example of what keeping me close in their hearts will achieve for the people. At first it seems that the Israelites do what God requested, devoting all things and all people to destruction (except Rahab and her family). After an unexpected setback at their next target, the city of Ai, YHWH informs Joshua that one of the Israelites has broken faith with God by not keeping the ban; he took some of the devoted items for personal gain. It is this breach, this "unwise" deed, that is responsible, apparently, for the defeat suffered at Ai. Joshua moves quickly to correct the situation and Achan, the transgressor, along with his family, are stoned and burned by "all Israel" (Joshua 7). Afterward YHWH "turned from his burning anger" (Josh 7:26).

How can the wisdom of God include the total destruction of a people, you ask? I know the notion that God sides only with particular members of God's own creation is a concept difficult for you moderns to reconcile with your understanding of a universal god. There are many possible ways, mostly inadequate, of coping with this dissonance: The Canaanites are the "bad guys" and deserve what they get. (But the idea that an entire people can be characterized as evil or as sinners obviously has dire consequences in today's world.) How about: The ancient Israelite god was just that, the god of Israel, and it was his "job" to protect "his" people? (Then why, you may ask, give the book that contains this story any credence as a source for a more universal salvation?) Or try this: In this depiction of God's might and commitment the people for whom it is originally written found great comfort, and a model for their own commitment to God's principles? Or, somewhat differently, the book of Joshua represents the early growing pains of a difficult transition, for both God and this people? Tough issues. Any single answer risks trivializing the challenges they pose.

What I suggest can be said with integrity is that the stories of Joshua and the people struggling to gain the land are also stories of the experience of a people to live responsibly within the commitments they make. Israel goes on to achieve many more victories under the leadership of Joshua (see Joshua 12 for a summary), but they fail to abolish entirely the temptation to stray posed by Canaanites. In fact, the continued presence of these people will prove a perennial stumbling block for Israel in its relationship with YHWH.

When the fighting finally dwindles, the tribes divvy up the land (Joshua 15–21), spreading out over a territory comprising the Carmel area in the north to the Negev in the South, west to the Mediterranean and east to just across the Jordan River. Joshua gives a final admonition to the people, reminding them of all the promises God has kept on behalf of the people. Once the territories are allotted, Joshua presents the people with a choice, irrevocable once made: Worship YHWH or choose otherwise. Should they choose YHWH, Joshua counsels them to remain true to the law they received at Sinai, especially as it pertains to exclusive worship of YHWH, because such loyalty will ensure God's continued presence and graciousness. If they fail in this commitment, Joshua correctly warns them, they "will perish from this good land" (Josh 23:13). With one voice the people vow their allegiance to the LORD (Josh 24:15-18). As you will see, that was the easy part; loyalty gets trickier once the honeymoon is over.

9. Samson among the Judges

Although you might think that once the tribes enter the "promised land," defeat many of the peoples of the land, and settle down into their apportioned territories they will be able to flourish in peace, such is not the case. The period between the settlement in (or conquering of) the land and the monarchy (called the period of the judges and related in the book of Judges), is marked by a violent and seemingly unbreakable cycle of disobedience (against God), retribution (by God), return (to God), and salvation (by God). The first phase of the cycle is initiated with the phrase "The Israelites d[o] what was evil in the sight of the LORD . . ." (e.g., Judg 6:1a), and God then manifests the retributive phase of the cycle by giving Israel over into the hands of their enemies, the most vexatious of whom are the Philistines. Typically the Israelites, after much suffering, would cry out to God and God would provide a named hero (called a judge) from among the people, a man (such as Gideon, Judges 6–8) or even a woman (Deborah, Judges 4), who through courage and wisdom would defeat Israel's enemies. And then the cycle begins again.

We can sample one of those stories here. Samson (Judges 13–16) is something of an unusual judge in that, to my dismay, he lacks wisdom (though not courage, to be sure). Although a Nazirite (one committed to God's service from birth), he is brash and arrogant and seems destined to lead his people into danger rather than away from it. Still, he is not the first character to prove that God can work wonders through fools and unscrupulous types who pay no mind to my call (remember—or look up—what Joseph says to his brothers in Gen 50:20). Also unique to Samson's judgeship, God seems to commission him to save Israel from the Philistines before, rather than in response to, the requisite phase of repentance on the part of the people. Such variety! Be on the watch for it.

Samson is born, in true hero fashion, of a union between his seemingly barren mother, a clueless father, and some intervention from YHWH himself (Judges 13, perhaps reminiscent of the strange story in Gen 6:1-4). He grows up to exhibit extraordinary, even supernatural strength (not unlike Hercules of Greek mythology). Throughout his life Samson seems more interested in chasing women (a penchant I have often warned against in the book of Proverbs), flouting his Nazirite vows, and avenging petty assaults on his honor than in doing his job of checking the Philistines. It is especially his weakness for women that gets him and his family into trouble. One day, for example, while traveling in a nearby village, just adjacent to Philistine territory, he is attracted to a Philistine woman and demands that his parents "get her" for him (Judg 14:2). His parents are deeply troubled that he wants a wife from among the "foreign others," but what they don't know (and neither, apparently, does Samson) is that this is all part of God's plan to establish a pretext to act against the Philistines because of their oppression of the Israelites. During the wedding feast Samson, in an audacious display of greed (another character trait that makes me flinch [Bar 3:17-18]), makes a bet with the Philistine guests that they each must pay him two lavish garments if they cannot solve his riddle. He is infuriated when his wife tells her family the answer to the riddle and, compelled by YHWH's spirit, he kills thirty men from the Philistine city of Ashkelon, thus paying his guests from the spoil of his killing spree.

Samson spends the remainder of his life inflicting damage on Israel's enemies, the Philistines. Although he is able to commit quite a bit of violence there is little evidence that Israel experiences any real peace during Samson's rule (in fact, at one point his own people try to turn him in to the Philistines, fearing reprisals for all the harm he has caused [Judges 15]). Equally troubling is the fact that he never unleashes his violent tendencies except to avenge his pride, usually bruised by his own foolishness in combination with the doings of one of the women he insists on getting involved with. Even up to the last moment of his life he has evidently not learned his lesson on this score. His love for another Philistine woman, Delilah, leads to the uncovering of the secret of his strength, which resides in the symbol of his Nazirite vows: his unshorn head of hair. After Delilah takes scissors to his hair (are you really to believe that any man of average intelligence can be "nagged" enough to reveal such a secret to a woman? [Judg 16:15-16]) he is captured by the Philistines, his eyes are gouged out, and he is put to work in a Philistine prison. His last act of revenge is to use his God-given power (the Philistines apparently fail to keep his hair trimmed in prison) to pull down the house of the Philistine god, Dagon, upon all inside it, killing himself in the process. It may have been a life devoid of discernment, but if the goal is to torment Israel's enemies, it is not without success. Is that the goal? Or do you think this is a campfire story about one of Israel's mythic superheroes?

10. Ruth, Naomi, and their Kin

Ruth, a woman from Moab (Israel's neighbor and quasi-enemy across the Jordan), is one of the few woman in the Bible who might be considered a genuine heroine, but not in the grand sense of a Deborah or Judith. On a more intimate level Ruth proves herself noble, loyal, and discerning, perhaps not unlike the woman praised in Proverbs 31: a woman truly after my own heart. On a larger historical level Ruth is remembered as the great-grandmother of King David. That familial connection accounts for her story's placement between the Book of Judges and 1 Samuel (which recounts the rise of the monarchy) in the Christian canons (Jews place it elsewhere).

The story of Ruth, which takes place during the period of the judges (Ruth 1:1), is a nice counterpoint to the theme of disobedience that prevails throughout the book of Judges. Israelites learn something about loyalty and obedience from this foreign woman who pledges herself to YHWH and to her Israelite mother-in-law, Naomi: ". . . your people shall be my people, and your God my God . . ." (Ruth 1:16b). She takes this oath after Naomi's husband and two sons die, leaving the older woman outside her homeland with two daughters-in-law and no way to care for them. One of the daughters goes back to her own people in Moab, but Ruth, despite Naomi's urging to the contrary, insists on returning to Judah with her mother-in-law. The generosity of this impulse is brought into sharp focus when we remember that Naomi, a woman past childbearing age and with no immediate family, is headed for destitution; Ruth is thus knowingly taking on herself such a fate.

When the two return to Bethlehem (which, ironically, translates as "house of bread"), the women of the village are moved by Naomi's sight and plight, saying among themselves, "Is this Naomi?" She responds that her name is no longer Naomi ("pleasant"), but rather Mara ("bitter"). Ruth proves as good as her vow and sets to work securing a meager sustenance for the women by gleaning the fields—as is her right according to Torah (see Lev 19:9-10; Deut 24:19-22)—of a wealthy man named Boaz, who also happens to be a distant relative of Naomi's dead husband. Boaz takes notice of her, treats her well, and ensures she is safe in his fields, and that she returns home at night with sacks full of grain. When her mother-in-law learns in whose fields Ruth had been gleaning, Naomi concocts a scheme that seems to involve some kind of sexual enticement (Ruth 3:1-5), the result of which is that Boaz will offer to wed Ruth, thus ensuring protection for both women. Ruth obeys Naomi—up to a point—and then improvises; the plan succeeds, except that Boaz needs to remove the obstacle of a nearer kin who has the first right of refusal of Ruth's hand. The nearer kin, at the mercy of some clever planning by Boaz, foregoes his right to marry Ruth as well as his option on a piece of land, heretofore unmentioned, that Naomi needs to sell. In nothing short of a fairytale ending Ruth and Boaz marry and have a son, Obed. The women of the village rejoice with Naomi, who can once again claim the legacy evoked by her name.

The Monarchic Period (Just pre-1000–587 B.C.E.)

11. Samuel and Saul (Pre-1000 B.C.E.)

The complexity of the period between the death of the specially-appointed Joshua and the choice of the first king is well represented by the stories just sampled from the period of the judges. The problems of leadership are made visible in the series of individuals appointed to deal with some episode but leaving the group headless for the next crisis. The other features of the period—which kingship will seek to remedy—are the threats to Israelites from external enemies (though by the end it is impossible to blame foreigners for what goes wrong) and the evident lack of unity of the tribal groups (ended temporarily only when the eleven tribes engage lone Benjamin in deadly civil war). The rule of the judges runs up against the start of monarchy (related in 1 Samuel) and includes among its named heroes Eli and Samuel, who have other roles as well. Samuel is the first prophet since Moses to be sketched in detail. We meet him before his birth, so to speak, as he is both fervently desired and prenatally given over by his mother Hannah to serve with the Elide priests at Shiloh, later to participate in some sort of circuit-judge ministry from there (1 Samuel 1–3). It is to the judge Samuel that Israel's elders come to request a king, prompted ostensibly by the catastrophic loss of the ark to the Philistines under the leadership of Eli's sons and more directly by the evident corruption of Samuel's sons, whom he has (quite anomalously) appointed to be judges themselves (1 Samuel 4–7). The people's request, its relay to God by Samuel, and the reply of YHWH are complex and somewhat undecidable, but I will suggest that it is the manner of the communication that sours the project rather than the request itself, which after all had been anticipated in legislation (Deuteronomy 17). Though God has been serving as Israel's king, the people leap over the divine incumbent to talk to the prophet about a replacement. And though God's language of feeling rejected seems clear as we watch Samuel hear those divine feelings articulated, the prophet does not deliver that reply of God specifically to the people, but obscures it by a rather unnuanced "yes" back from God.

God, willing to try human kingship even if affronted by it in some aspect, indicates Saul, son of Kish, a Benjaminite, to be the first king. Saul responds at first less than enthusiastically. But he is crowned and approved and even does a deed of deliverance for the people of Jabesh in Gilead that indicates his leadership potential (1 Samuel 8–11). The multiple events surrounding the choice of Saul as proto-king are climaxed as the prophet Samuel summarizes the situation. He says, in effect: Kingship can work if people and king do the one thing needful, which is carefully to heed God's word; lacking such a commitment and behavior, the monarchic enterprise will crash and all players will be swept away together (1 Samuel 12). But if such a start seems promising, shortly thereafter Saul fails cosmically to hear well and heed carefully and is fired after two major miscues involving his leadership in cult and war (1 Samuel 13–15). By now, however, Saul seems to have warmed to his task and he refuses to vacate the royal post. God does not insist, but simply walks around Saul to select young David of Bethlehem in Judah, whom Samuel anoints as king. Without knowing that David is his God-designated successor, Saul learns of the young man's skills and invites him to the palace to be musician and armor-bearer (1 Samuel 16). Thus begins a fatal pattern in which the old king unwittingly summons his nemesis and opponent to take over the royal position. Unable to fight the Philistine giant, Saul arms David to do it (1 Samuel 17). When people approve David's prowess, Saul turns instantly and deeply jealous. Saul arranges betrothals between his daughters and David, episodes that boomerang, leaving Saul at a disadvantage in one way or another. Saul's son Jonathan becomes David's ally, a situation that turns Saul against David all the more (1 Samuel 18–20).

After a series of complex interactions David flees the household of Saul and goes out on his own. Saul, who now seems to be spending all his royal time and energy tracking David, continues to alienate his own people from a loyalty he can scarcely afford to lose. Though Saul seems to be pursuing David, the initiative and advantage slowly reverse, and it becomes possible to see that David is skillfully hunting, even baiting his royal opponent (1 Samuel 21–26). The stories turn to the various dangers involved as these two kings struggle to disable each other, but also to refrain from raising their hands against God's anointed. That David is YHWH's anointed is clear to him and to readers, if not necessarily to Saul, who plausibly sees him as a mere upstart. Saul continues to resist the clear information he has been given about the abortive termination of his own dynastic line and speaks of his son Jonathan in terms of succession. But it is not to be. As the story of Israel's first king winds toward its end the Philistines, troublesome at least since the days of the judge Samson, mass in great numbers, striking deep fear into Saul (1 Samuel 28). Terrified of them, panicked by the long silence of God, and wanting someone to tell him what to do, he violates his own order (and the ethos of the narrator who is telling the story) and asks a medium to put him in touch with the realm of the dead. She is hesitant to do so but proficient when the king insists, and she raises up the prophet Samuel from the dead. Saul asks his old mentor Samuel for advice, but Samuel insists that Saul has already been told what he must to do, words the king has ignored, Samuel hints. Samuel does disclose to Saul two pieces of information arguably new to him: that on the morrow Saul and sons will be joining Samuel in the land of the dead, and that it is YHWH who has promoted David's cause. Stunned by that news, Saul topples over, weakened by his fasting. The medium feeds the king, strengthening him to face his death bravely, which he does next day on Mount Gilboa (1 Samuel 31). Though some see Saul's death as ignominious—the dread presence of the Philistines prompting him to fall on his own sword—it is actually one of the king's better moments. The circumstances and meaning of the royal death immediately become controversial. The Philistines rejoice and expose Saul's corpse to dishonor, while the loyal and mindful people of Jabesh rescue the body, burn and bury it, and mourn Saul. A foreigner claims that he killed the old king, thinking that David, to whom he makes the boast, will reward him. Without pursuing in detail the question of exactly how the man came upon Saul's royal regalia, David executes him and sings and teaches a beautiful poem about Saul and Jonathan, itself as enigmatic as the story we have of them (2 Samuel 1).

12. David and his Household (Tenth–Ninth Centuries B.C.E.)

If I said previously that Moses is the hero of the Hebrew Bible, I must now counter that David runs a close second. Like the story of Moses, David's narrative is pretty well dispersed throughout the Bible, at least by reference and allusion. So I will need now to be schematic and sum up his achievements in a more synthetic than text-driven way. The basic narrative events are most visible in 1 Samuel, where we see David chosen as king by God, anointed by Samuel, and resisted by Saul. But after Saul is dead his own clan of Judah make David king and the rest of the tribes agree a few years later. David's rule as king is told in 2 Samuel, with his death and decision that his son Solomon will succeed him told at the start of 1 Kings. David is also mentioned as either the author or the occasion of a number of psalms (nearly half of the 150 psalms are headed "of" or "to" David) and he is typically understood to figure in others (e.g., Psalms 2, 18, 97, 110). Also, the king (David or one of his heirs) is praised in several other psalms.

From that material and from elsewhere to be noted in the Bible let me summarize David's achievements, first the positive ones and then those that may appear more dubious to you. David's main political accomplishment is twofold. First, the credit for establishing "the nation" (anachronistic as that term may be), goes to David. Though Saul is the first named king, David's efforts to unify the people under his kingship, to select a city for his center (Jerusalem), to build a palace, to consolidate relations with the nations nearby in one way or another, to defeat or subdue the Philistines (and other foes), to beget offspring, to appoint a core of administrators— all these mark David as the first unifying leader since Joshua (2 Samuel 2–9). David's second political accomplishment has to be the founding of a relatively stable dynasty, one that is to last almost unbroken for more than four hundred years. In fact the house of David, whose rule seems to break off at the time of exile in the sixth century, actually picks up momentum as a symbol of or aspiration for effective leadership and survives in the many texts that bespeak a longing for an anointed hero or messiah, a particular edition of which is refracted in some of the language about Jesus the Christ (i.e., the anointed one) in the Christian period. Even if, as historians are wont to suggest, David's kingdom emerged during a leadership vacuum shared by the large surrounding empires (Egypt, Assyria-Babylon, the western Anatolian-Macedonian-Greek enterprises), emerge it did and survive it did with David's heirs for quite some time. You may even think, with some historians, that the monarchy is responsible for more harm than good, a point certain prophets will hint at. But it seems that without such stability we might now be rehearsing quite a different story!

David's religious achievement stressed in 1 Chronicles (a later narration of the events of the Judean monarchy) is undercut somewhat by the less valorizing narrative of 2 Samuel. Both texts suggest that David, like any other ancient Near Eastern king, longs to build a temple to honor the deity and to make visible his own royal sovereignty; but it was not to be. God and David's prophet Nathan assure the king that Solomon will be the temple builder. But the narrator of Chronicles lovingly portrays David as gathering the materials in readiness, as selecting the site for the shrine, and as organizing the vast and complex cult so that Solomon's job is made easier for him. In that sense David's contribution to cult is made central. David's spiritual achievement, if I may nuance the realm usually referred to as religious, is depicted throughout the biblical sources. David is shown to be an intimate of God in somewhat the same way as Moses. Compared with his predecessor Saul, who has no apparent access to God, David communicates— and is communicated with—readily and easily. David remains close to God even when his sins are great, a fidelity not seen in his son Solomon, who starts out well with God and then seems to become distracted and disloyal. David is said to have a heart like God's, or to be a man after God's own heart, i.e., of God's own choosing. So whatever else may need to be said, David's capacity to remain a friend of God is perhaps his key quality.

It cannot have been so easy, since David's sins are neither small nor few. I will leave aside whatever case might be made for a certain disloyalty on his part to Saul; you may investigate that story in 1 Samuel. As David consolidates his rule, various of his erstwhile opponents seem to die suddenly and conveniently, whether by a royal nudge or nod is not so clear. But David clearly crosses the line when he appropriates Bathsheba, wife of one of his own comrades (Uriah), to satisfy his own desire; once she has conceived their child, David manipulates mightily—and unsuccessfully—to shift suspicion from himself. Uriah is set up both by David and by the king's right-hand man Joab to be killed in a war, and David takes possession of the widow Bathsheba with no apparent qualm (2 Samuel 11–12). But God is disturbed at David's behavior and rebukes him through the prophet Nathan, marking the king's sin by the death of the child adulterously and treacherously conceived. David acknowledges his sin and intercedes for the child, a plea not granted by God. This cardinal taking by David—his greed affecting all those around him—is next made visible in his own family (2 Samuel 13–19). His sons fight each other, are involved in the rape of their sister Tamar, implicate their father in their deeds of violence, and bring the moral pathology to full bloom in a coup organized against David by his son Absalom. Though the young prince fails, ultimately, to drive his father off the throne, he comes close enough, and as David lies on his deathbed another son, Adonijah, jumps the gun and seizes power, that act reversed in Solomon's favor only by the combined intervention of Bathsheba and Nathan (and whoever else you think shapes deeds!).

A bold human being, a great heart, sometimes a sinful man, surely an intimate of God: all these descriptions and more suit King David.

13. Solomon, Jeroboam, Ahijah of Shiloh

The succession to David's throne is contested, and not only by his sons. The narrative of transition (told in 1 Kings 1–2) suggests (with some ambiguity) that Solomon is the son designated by David to succeed to the throne in Jerusalem. Solomon's narrative lacks the depth and intensity seen in the stories of his two predecessors, but there is still plenty to ponder. Solomon's activities are summarized in 1 Kings 1–11, in 2 Chronicles 1–9, and a bit more obliquely in the many proverbs he is said to have authored (the book of Proverbs contains some of them), in Ecclesiastes/Qoheleth (which purports to be reminiscences of David's son), and in Wisdom of Solomon, also attributed to him. The main storyline gives Solomon huge credit for two other things. First, he is the builder of the Temple in Jerusalem (the first Temple, or Solomon's Temple), which stands from the end of the tenth to the beginning of the sixth century. To build a temple is a royal prerogative, and though David had hoped and even planned to do that honorific task himself, God defers it until the next generation. Though 1 Chronicles suggests that David gets Solomon started well by gathering and stockpiling the materials, the account in Kings details the achievement as Solomon's, giving careful attention to and hence great stress upon the significance of the deed. The building is described as lavish in every way, beautiful, ornate, complex, well-suited to worship of Israel's God. Executed by Hiram of Tyre, the first Temple is made of cedar, studded with precious metals, softened by beautifully-figured hangings, and made a shelter for the old ark of God and host for the other implements needed for worship. The construction of a permanent place for God's name (which is one way the Temple is described) makes Solomon an exemplary king.

Solomon's second achievement, if that is the right word, is his reputation for wisdom. When God asks Solomon to name what he wishes to be given, Solomon asks for wisdom and thus gains all that accompanies this deep quality, myself included. Solomon's wisdom is literally proverbial and fabled. He is credited with many gnomic sayings, and stories about his sagacity are told, including one where he seems to read two desperate women and a baby well (1 Kings 3:16-28), and another where the Queen of Sheba acknowledges his wealth—both intangible and tangible (1 Kings 10:1-11). Wisdom—Sophia—is the consort and advisor of kings—or I am willing that this be one of my many modes of presence, and Solomon's heart inclines toward my gifts for some time. Solomon also expands the territory of his nation, builds up the city Jerusalem, and leaves significant architectural achievements elsewhere in the land he controls.

The underside, visible as well in the 1 Kings narrative about Solomon (chs. 1–11), is suggested by an uncertainty in his succession (had David really promised that Solomon was his heir or was he manipulated by Bathsheba and Nathan?), a violence that attends his early reign, a hint that the vast expanse of his building projects costs him a swath of northern cities, and the note that his reorganization of the twelve tribes (efficient for purposes of taxation) brings at least some of the tribes under mandatory labor and crushing levies. The storyteller is more blunt about the multiple marriages that Solomon enters, relationships that distract him from the worship of YHWH as prescribed in Deuteronomy. By the end of his reign Solomon suits poorly the king described in the legislation that provides for a king (Deuteronomy 17), since he has acquired money, horses, and women and is in danger of "returning the people to Egypt," one way or another. God chastises Solomon for false worship by the end of his reign and registers the intent to break off at least part of the kingdom from the Davidic line, not in Solomon's lifetime but in that of his son Rehoboam.

And so it goes. Rehoboam, not conspicuously attended by wisdom or Wisdom, speaks and acts foolishly when seeking the assent of the tribes to his reign—a question, by the way, that will not be asked so obviously again by a Davidic heir. Ahijah of Shiloh, one of the several prophets who begin now importantly to dot the scene, gestures by a dramatic rending of a robe that Ephraimite Jeroboam (an adversary of Solomon's) is to be given kingship over ten of the tribes (1 Kings 12). The diminishment of the Davidic heritage (also known as the splitting of the kingdom into northern Israel and southern Judah) is thus legitimated by divine word and by prophetic action. But almost at once the newly crowned Jeroboam commits a sin so egregious in the eyes of his southern (Jerusalem-based) chronicler that it remains the standard of infidelity for generations to come. Jeroboam, thinking in practical terms, decides that for his people to go up to Jerusalem for worship will undermine his own sovereignty. He thus establishes new sacrifice sites at Dan and Bethel, erects worship apparatus that includes golden bovines, allows non-legitimate priests access to ministry, and shuffles the liturgical calendar. So Jeroboam stands condemned, not so much for being a king of Israel as for being the instigator of false worship that will dog his people throughout their two-hundred-year existence. Suitably within the symbol system of the teller of these tales, Jeroboam's eldest son dies despite the efforts of the royal wife and mother to get help for him from the once-favorably-disposed but now disapproving Ahijah (1 Kings 13–14). A second son succeeds his father, but briefly, and the first of the very few dynasties the northern kingdom of Israel will enjoy is ended with only two members. A period of three successive and chaotic reigns ensues before the accession of the dynasty known as Omrides. In the meantime Rehoboam and his heirs continue to sit on the throne in the impoverished and diminished Judah.

14. Ahab, Jezebel, Elijah, and Elisha (Ninth Century B.C.E.)

Ahab's father, Omri, contributes his name to a small but highly successful dynasty that rules the northern kingdom of Israel from the early to the mid-ninth century. According to 1 Kings 16, King Omri founded Samaria, the capital of the northern kingdom. This is the only information about Omri related in the biblical text, but scholars have learned from extra-biblical sources that the House of Omri ruled over an internationally significant kingdom.

1 Kings is not nearly so taciturn regarding King Ahab. As typical of the description given to the rulers of the northern kingdom, Ahab's reign is denigrated: "Ahab son of Omri did evil in the sight of the LORD more than all who were before him" (1 Kgs 16:30). This "evil" pertains specifically to Ahab's spousal arrangement. He marries Jezebel, a Phoenician princess

who (naturally enough) worships the god of her people, Baal, and apparently influences Ahab to do likewise (a point made about Solomon as well). Ahab builds a temple for Baal in Samaria (though it is not surprising that his wife would want a temple dedicated to her god in her new home). Needless to say, this is unacceptable behavior for YHWH's king, and it "provoke[s] the anger of the LORD" (1 Kgs 16:33).

Elijah, YHWH's prophet, delivers the message to Ahab that, as a result of his infidelity and disobedience, the land will suffer a severe drought (1 Kings 17). Elijah has to go into hiding to protect himself from the wrath of Ahab, and God feeds him and sends him to a poor widow in Zarephath, where he performs some amazing miracles in the name of the LORD, the most dramatic being the resuscitation of the widow's dead son (1 Kgs 17:20-24). These are only the first of many wonders performed by Elijah and his successor, Elisha (introduced in 1 Kgs 19:19 and extending as far as 2 Kings 9). In an audacious display of raw power that recalls the ancient mythical battles between the gods of old, Elijah challenges the prophets of Baal to a contest meant to prove once and for all that only YHWH is God. Four hundred fifty prophets of Baal assemble before the people of Israel in a contest against the lone Elijah and the sovereign YHWH. Elijah challenges them to offer a burnt offering without using fire; like Elijah, the Baal prophets will have to rely on divine power alone to ignite the sacrifice. Both sides slaughter and prepare a bull for sacrifice and place it on the altar. After much wailing and praying, the prophets of Baal fail (or rather, their god does). You've probably already guessed that YHWH comes through in sensational fashion: "Fire of the LORD fell and consumed the burnt offering, the wood, the stones, and the dust . . ." (1 Kgs 18:38). Rain follows the fire, finally breaking the drought. This doesn't spell good news for the prophets of Baal, though, who pay with their lives for their "wrong" devotion.

Jezebel is furious at the news of the demise of her prophets, and she seeks Elijah's life, causing him to flee to Mount Horeb (sometimes called Mount Sinai) where, like Moses, he has a close encounter with YHWH (1 Kgs 19:11-18). Elijah is commissioned to anoint three persons: his successor (Elisha), an Aramean king (Hazael), and a replacement for the Omride rulers (Jehu), tasks that are accomplished later, if not sooner. After all of this one would think that Ahab had learned his lesson about what it means to be YHWH's anointed. Instead his deeds once again find him in conflict with Elijah: Ahab covets the vineyard of one of his own citizens, a man from Jezreel called Naboth. When Naboth refuses, as is his right in law, to sell the land to Ahab, the king whines to his wife, Jezebel, who concocts a successful scheme to have Naboth falsely accused of blasphemy and subsequently put to death. When Ahab takes possession of the land, Elijah delivers the LORD's verdict that Ahab will pay with his life for this deed (1 Kgs 21:17-19). Indeed he does, dying in a battle against the king of Aram (1 Kings 22). Above and beyond the particularities, this tale is a good snapshot of what goes wrong with the monarchy in general, at least according to many of the prophets. As power is centralized and institutionalized it becomes too absolute; the rulers of Israel forget the real source of that power and consequently the gap between the powerful and the powerless grows dangerously wide. The later prophets—listen for Amos, Hosea, Isaiah, and Micah—will be especially effective at exposing this violation of YHWH's precepts.

Elisha's cycle of stories reads quite well as a reflection of the consequences of this power differential. Many of the stories Elisha dominates are concerned with the poor and marginalized, those who seem to have no recourse except the miraculous deeds Elisha performs for them. Some of these dispossessed are identified as bands of prophets, of which Elisha seems to be some kind of leader. Like his predecessor he prophesies to leaders, raises a young boy from the dead, and feeds people from scant resources (2 Kings 3–4). In actual deeds he may even exceed the greatness of Elijah, who, when carried off into the heavens in a chariot, bestows on Elisha a "double portion" of his spirit (2 Kings 2).

What about Jezebel, you are wondering, the apparent instigator of much of the trouble? After a coup by King Jehu (finally anointed, as Elijah had been ordered, though by an anonymous prophet), a defiant Jezebel is tossed from the window of her palace where the horses trample upon her and the dogs eat her flesh (in accordance with the prophecy of Elijah in 1 Kings 21). Ahab's son and grandson as well as all the potential rulers of Israel and Judah are also slaughtered in the coup (2 Kings 9–10). So ends the Omride dynasty, one of the most heinous from the perspective of the biblical authors, though not necessarily so according to most worldly standards, which would credit it as one of the more prosperous periods in Israel's history.

15. Amos, Hosea, and the Jehu Dynasty (Eighth Century B.C.E.)

All that seems wrong about the Omrides—their apparent capitulation to the foreign ways of the Phoenician court, the aggressive patterns of land management so at odds with the sense of ancestral heritage held as a gift from YHWH, the prominence of the Baal culture in both politics and religion—receives scathing critique from the northern prophets. Elijah, commissioned to anoint a new king and new dynasty to deal with these matters, leaves his successor Elisha to tap an anonymous prophet on the shoulder to do the actual dangerous commissioning of Jehu. Before getting to the specifics of Jehu's rule and that of his four heirs it is time to name directly a situation that the biblical storyteller tends to understress. If the whole story of origins lying outside the biblical storyline could be told, it would feature the reemergence into activity of the huge empires surrounding the small proto-Jewish people. Egypt (to the southwest) has already been part of the story, as would be the Anatolian/Hittite presence to the northwest (which will emerge later as Macedonia and Greece). The monarchic part of the story is more tangled with the Mesopotamian monsters, Assyria to the northeast and Babylon (and later Persia), roughly southeast. These greedy entities threaten, dominate, and eventually absorb all the smaller peoples that have come into being while the giant empires (Egypt, Assyria, Babylonia) have slept in weakness. They will largely determine what happens, at least on the macroscopic scale. The biblical storyteller who relates to you these centuries and generations, dynasties and monarchic characters tends to cast the fate of Judah and Israel in moral terms—not inaccurate, but not quite complete. The large empires are determined to control trade routes along the Mediterranean (linking themselves to each other) and demand goods in order to keep their imperial machinery humming. The task of the leadership of Israel and Judah seems to consist at this moment of a variety of strategies to keep at least a modicum of independence. We can let the northern prophets Amos and Hosea each show us a distinctive aspect of it.

But first Jehu. I told you that he is envisioned as a reformer in the spirit of Elijah and Elisha, and that, once anointed king, he assassinates the whole house of Omrides, including the notorious Jezebel, wife of one king (Ahab) and mother of two (Ahaziah and Jehoram). Some seventy potential heirs to the throne of Israel are killed at Jehu's whim, along with forty-two survivors of the slain king of Judah. An under-remembered interval of six years ensues in Judah, when Athaliah, daughter of Ahab and Jezebel of Israel, wife of King Jehoram and mother of King Ahaziah (both of Judah) rules as queen from Jerusalem, until she, too, is slain in a bloody coup and a young Davidic Joash put in place, thanks to the offices of the priest Jehoida. But to return a final time to the troubles in the north: During the one hundred years of rule by Jehu's descendants, with the power of Assyria threatening ever more relentlessly, the monarchy strengthens, or at least grows more centrally powerful. The Jehuide kings reach out for more produce to hand over to their overlords as well as for their own enjoyment. More ancestral land goes into overdrive production, passing out of the enfeebled hands of its erstwhile owners to fall under royal control. (Recall Naboth). The gap between the few elites and the many others widens, and the circumstances of the lives of the poor grow more dire. Amos, first of the "book-writing prophets," appearing suddenly on the scene in Israel, addresses this scandalous gap with oracles, riddles, and questions, harsh imagery and strong certainties, making clear his sense that the kingdom of Israel has already gone past its survival date. Amos has a famous clash with a Bethel-shrine priest, Amaziah, and indirectly with Jehuide King Jeroboam II, where the priest threatens to hurl the prophet out of the neighborhood for his supposed words of treason against the king. Amos, with little left to lose, claims divine sanction for his vision and his language. As you read the short text that bears his name you will likely spot evidence of its layered growth. That is (as will happen in the case of virtually all the writing prophets), the preaching of eighth-century Amos is enhanced and enriched by later passages that dialogue with and soften his more definite language about the end of God's project in Israel. The palimpsestic (layered) quality of such prophetic preaching helps show the esteem in which the prophetic words are held while at the same time giving evidence of the mystery and malleability of YHWH's speech with and care for people.

The problem you can see most helpfully in Hosea (while not disregarding his concern for the social injustices to which Amos also calls attention) is the problem of false religion. This is a complex situation. It helps, I think, if you realize that all peoples of the ancient Near Eastern neighbor hood worshiped in a multiplicity of ways: many manifestations of deity, with tangible objects to assist worship, in various sites, with diverse intermediaries, and with a richness of rites. Over time, and thanks to prophets like those just named, there is a growing sense (suffusing Deuteronomy, Joshua, Judges, Samuel, and Kings as well as certain "writing" prophets) that what is demanded and desired for Judah and Israel is something more simple, less embodied, more centralized, less multipolar. The shorthand for that movement is "YHWH alone," a slogan, if we can call it that, that celebrates the sovereignty of one God and mandates cult that is carried out formally and officially, at least, at the Temple in Jerusalem under the management of legitimate authorities (Davidic kings while they last, and Aaronic and Levitical priests). The various prophets we are dealing with here struggle to help people see the value of such change, but they will have an uphill battle. The prophet Hosea, preaching shortly after Amos and just before the collapse of the kingdom of Israel, boldly laces his language with imagery from the Ugaritic-Canaanite cult and culture that is on the wane, reworking some of it for the YHWH religion and making the rest seem corrupt. Hosea's language of marriage infidelities and of woes besieging parents and children, and his vivid images of sickness and health, all struggle to show the "new" Yahwistic religion adequately. In the prophets' eyes the kings have long since substantially abandoned their basic charge of helping people stay faithful to the God of the tradition, and this fact makes inevitable what in fact happens around the year 721, roughly two hundred years after the split of the northern tribes from the Davidic-Solomonic kingdom. The Assyrians, long tired of various other treaty arrangements with the kings living in Israel's capital Samaria, besiege and defeat the kingdom, exiling the Israelite people and in fact replacing them with others relocated from some other spot in the empire. The story of Jonah, with its strong ambivalence about the capacity of Assyria for God's mercy, makes a certain amount of sense in this phase, as does perhaps the story of Tobit and his family.

16. Ahaz, Hezekiah, (First) Isaiah, Micah (Seventh–Sixth Centuries B.C.E.)

The story of the two kingdoms, Israel and Judah, continues to toggle from North to South (at least in the book of 2 Kings) until the collapse of Israel, which, as I have just suggested, comes shortly after the time of Hosea. The last decades of the northern kingdom, though shadowed by increasingly persistent pressure from the Assyrian empire, seem more troublesome to the eighth-century prophets for their contribution to an increasingly radical social inequity. The prophets do speak boldly against various foreign nations and cultures, and part of what they are condemning is the sort of Levantine or Mediterranean power politics that makes it difficult for monarchs to resist the agricultural intensification that impoverishes most of the population and enriches the few while providing tribute of one kind or another for the hungry empire to the northeast. One episode of which we are told—involving both Israel and Judah and their two kings (Pekah in the north and Ahaz in the south)—comes as a desperate and threatening move on the part of Pekah and his ally (the king of Aramean Damascus) to induce King Ahaz of Judah to join in a coalition its founders think will threaten Assyria. Unusually, not only does 2 Kings hint at the episode (2 Kings 16), but the prophet Isaiah includes it as well (Isaiah 7). In the 2 Kings version King Ahaz simply invokes Assyrian help over the heads of his threatening peers and would-be allies. When traveling to Damascus, Ahaz becomes distracted by an altar he sees there, which he incorporates into the Jerusalem Temple, eliminating the one installed by Solomon (a deed the Kings narrator relates, surprisingly, without underlining its illegality). As the episode is related in Isaiah, that prophet warns Ahaz not to give in to the threats of his erstwhile peers, but to trust in the birth of a royal son, sign that Ahaz's line will survive, though his would-be coalition partners will disappear. In fact, the prophetic narrative even implies or allows the view that Ahaz's refusal to heed his prophet—he invokes Assyrian assistance instead of trusting God's—is instrumental in bringing the Assyrian giant into the neighborhood to the detriment of the northern kingdom. But in any case the storyteller in Kings concludes soberly the story of northern Israel, relating the devastating defeat of its capital city Samaria, detailing the exile of the population, and explaining how the replacement population—brought to the region from somewhere within the Assyrian empire—fails to worship God properly, despite a prophet to assist them in God's ways. From here on the story focuses on the last century or so (for some 135 years) of the southern kingdom of Judah.

Isaiah's long prophetic ministry, overlapping the final days before the fall of the north, continues in Judah, where the recalcitrant Ahaz is succeeded by his son King Hezekiah, an exemplary monarch not only in Chronicles (2 Chronicles 29–32, where kings tend to behave better) but even in Kings (2 Kings 18–20). The threat of absorption continues from Assyria, all the more since the survival of the southern kingdom simply presents a new opportunity and a fresh border for the powerful enemy to the northeast. In what is presented as a series of episodes Assyria draws threateningly near with one demand or another for Judah's capitulation. Isaiah insists that the monarchy (king and dynasty), the city Jerusalem, its Temple, and the people resist dealing with him, though Isaiah's stark demands seem foolish to many. Hezekiah, though tempted to aggression against Assyria, ultimately seems to have resisted coalitions or direct engagement with the big enemy. Though the Assyrian king comes right to the edge of the city—wreaking the sort of havoc in the hinterland that the prophet Micah bitterly decries as he and the rural population experience it—the city Jerusalem is spared, barely and miraculously. Micah's experience and words, somewhat at variance with those of Isaiah, remind all that rural life and ministry are not the same as urban, and he helps make clear the complexity of the phenomenon of prophecy, the many challenges of mediating the will of God into human language and experience. Prophets disagree, and legitimately so. Isaiah, though consistent about the futility of reliance upon any political arrangements with foreign nations, preaches insistently as well against social injustice. His language, strong and image-filled, seems to alternate between despair for the future and hope, or perhaps between his confidence in the long-range future and his disquiet about short-term prospects. Isaiah's last words to King Hezekiah, spoken to rebuke the king for displaying the contents of the royal treasury too freely to envoys from Babylon, tell of a future remote to Hezekiah when Babylon will be a place of exile for the king's descendants.

A last important note about Hezekiah, stressed more in 2 Chronicles than in 2 Kings, reminds us of the importance of proper worship, that responsibility that virtually all the kings (whether in the north or the south) seem strangely and consistently to flout, for whatever reasons. Hezekiah, most dutiful and creative reformer since Solomon, undertakes reconstruction (or repair) of the Temple and reform of the cult. Hezekiah's efforts are both destructive of the so-called foreign ways (worship that falls eventually outside the bounds of Yahwism) and constructive of what can be called nationalistic (YHWH alone) worship. Under his rule steps are envisioned toward strengthening worship in the Jerusalem Temple and making certain feasts to involve pilgrimages to that site, but not quite successfully or consistently carried out. The change of worship is not simple for people, and the coalescence of cultic behavior centered on YHWH alone does not come easily or quickly. Hezekiah is a major milestone along the way. However, his son and successor, Manasseh, reverses these policies and seals the fate of the Judean monarchy (2 Kings 21, mitigated a bit in 2 Chronicles 33).

17. Jeremiah, Nahum, Zephaniah, Habakkuk, Josiah, Huldah

What Manassah undoes, his grandson Josiah (639–609 B.C.E.) tries to repair. Perhaps the only king (not counting the peerless David and Solomon) more fondly remembered by the tradition than Hezekiah is Josiah. During a refurbishment of the LORD's Temple (2 Kings 22) supported by Josiah, the high priest Hilkiah finds a scroll of *torah* (or "teaching"). When this scroll is read out to King Josiah he tears his clothes (a traditional symbol of mourning). This scroll, containing God's teachings for the people, mysteriously lost and (some say suspiciously) found, makes it all too clear that both the people and the king have been unwittingly transgressing God's commands. When he tears his clothes Josiah is demonstrating his piety, insofar as he is genuinely grieved, even horrified, by this deep and persistent lapse. He well comprehends the weighty consequences of such pervasive disregard of all that YHWH had established with the early ancestors at the time of Moses.

Fearing the worst, the people in charge consult a prophetess named Huldah (one of the few female prophets named in the biblical tradition), and the word of the LORD that comes to her indicates it is too late to avoid consequences in Judah for the neglect of *torah;* but she also does not discourage Josiah from attempting to reform what he can. This obviously important scroll is never identified precisely, but because of the implied curses it contains for failure to commit to its spirit and accede to its precepts, as well as because of the specific reforms that Josiah enacts according to the demands of the scroll, many scholars assume it was some version of the book of Deuteronomy. Most prominent among the reforms is the complete eradication and annihilation of non-Yahwistic cults and priesthoods (2 Kings 23). On the positive side Josiah also centralizes worship in Jerusalem (building on what King Hezekiah had begun) and reinstates the Passover sacrifice, two other chief practices of Deuteronomy's law. For all this it is said of Josiah: "Before him there was no king like him, who turned to the LORD with all his heart, with all his soul, and with all his might, according to all the law of Moses . . ." (2 Kgs 23:25). King Josiah stands forth as a man attuned to my summons, a paragon of the essential link between wisdom and piety. Even so, as we will see, the "wickedness" of the people (kings included) is too great to be reversed.

But in the meantime Judah apparently enjoys a period of political and religious renewal (at least in Yahwistic terms). They are even able to shake off the yoke of Assyria for a time. Assyria becomes so weak and vulnerable, in fact, that it eventually falls (612 B.C.E.) to its "up and coming" neighbor to the south, Babylon. The small prophetic book of Nahum (another of the twelve "minor prophets," so called because their books are comparatively brief), celebrates Assyria's downfall, crediting the LORD with the victory. Using vivid and often brutal imagery (Nah 3:5–7), Nahum taunts Nineveh (capital of Assyria), claiming that the city is reaping what it has sown and (incorrectly) seeing the fall of Nineveh as the ultimate redemption of Judah. Egypt steps into the void left by the Assyrians and attempts to (re)control Judah and the surrounding territories. In 609 King Josiah dies fighting Egyptian aggression (2 Kgs 23:29).

For a country surrounded by much larger, stronger, and aggressive nations any rejoicing over the defeat of one of them is bound to be short-lived. After a few years of vassalage to the Egyptians, Judah comes under the control of the Babylonians. As it turns out, Babylon is no improvement over Assyria. So heavy, in fact, is the burden the Babylonians place on the Judahites that the book of the prophet Habakkuk (another minor prophet) is dedicated to pleading with God to do justly by vanquishing the Babylonians. Habakkuk boldly complains to God: "Why do you look on the treacherous, and are silent when the wicked swallow those more righteous than they?" (Hab 1:13b). YHWH responds that the faithful will be rewarded, but that the rise of the Chaldeans (another word for the Babylonians) is all a part of the divine plan, and indicates that in the end the empire will pay for its greed and overzealousness (ch. 2). While Habakkuk doesn't necessarily imply that God is raising up the Babylonians simply to punish Judah for their infidelity, it is not difficult to read that viewpoint from the writers of Kings and the "book prophets" (major and minor) who write about Judah's fate.

The history of the monarchy can be seen as a falling out of relationship, compounded by a progression into sin and rebelliousness, that inevitably culminates in the final execution of God's wrath, played out through God's instruments—first the Assyrians and then the Babylonians. It isn't as if they weren't warned! During this period (mid-to late 7th century), most prominent among the voices raised in admonition is that of Jeremiah, a major prophet who preaches from the reign of Josiah until the fall of Jerusalem to the Babylonians in 587 B.C.E. Another minor prophet, Zephaniah, also does his part to warn Judah of the upcoming disaster should they not repent and return to the LORD (Zeph 1:4-6). The voices of these two contemporary prophets are rather contradictory: irreversible destruction on the one hand but a chance to alter their fate on the other (Zeph 2:1-3; Jer 7:5-7). But if you have been reading carefully you will not find this the first ambivalence among those charged with care for YHWH's people. This paradox is an accurate reflection of the burden of prophetic calling. How unthinkable it must have been to preach a message completely devoid of hope, no matter how clear the signs!

Jeremiah is particularly creative in God's service, perhaps since his ministry lasts for some decades. There is relatively little to glean about the man himself from the book named for him, but perhaps more than we know about most prophets. He seems to have come from a priestly family in Anathoth, outside Jerusalem, a group that had contributed leaders before. As such he seems to have wielded some influence in the community, although the negativity of his message—he urges submission to Babylon—gets him into trouble, despite whatever prestige his background and reputation may have earned him. As you can appreciate, his advice seemed very unpatriotic, particularly to factions in the city Jerusalem that had other words for the ears of the four kings who succeed Josiah. Because the book contains so much language that recalls the exhortations of Deuteronomy, and because Jeremiah's primary theme is the idolatry of the people, many think he has to have been a supporter of Josiah's reforms (though he does not allude to them specifically). Insofar as Jeremiah is an accurate gauge of his society we can infer that the king's reforms do not much outlast his own reign, hence the need for God to commission another leader (Jeremiah 1) to the odious and apparently hopeless task (see Jer 7:27; 15:1).

Jeremiah finds his commission a tremendous burden, however committed to YHWH he may be. God forbids him to have a family (16:2), and God forbids him to pray for his people—intercession being a primary prophetic role (14:11). Jeremiah's friends become his enemies (20:10); he is more than once put in prison for making treasonous public statements that seem defeatist and disloyal (26:11; 38:1-6). On many occasions he expresses his dissatisfaction to God: "You will be in the right, O LORD, / when I lay charges against you; / but let me put my case against you" (12:1); "O LORD, you have enticed me, / and I was enticed; / you have over powered me, / and you have prevailed" (20:7a). Yet Jeremiah's loyalty and, ultimately, his trust in the LORD remain firm. In fact, so embedded is God's word in Jeremiah's heart that even when he may want to abandon his calling, he cannot do it (Jer 20:9). Unlike the core of Isaiah's message, which counsels the people to trust that YHWH will protect them against their enemies, Jeremiah's message is counter-intuitive: YHWH's protective shield over Zion is not an entitlement, not a given, not if the people continue in their so unjust and idolatrous ways (7:1-11). Such preaching is, as you can imagine, bound to make him unpopular (consider, for example, how resistant Americans would be during wartime to hearing that they deserve to be brutally defeated because they have not been faithful enough to God).

As unpopular as his message might have been at the time, Jeremiah's words are kept for posterity because in the end his view of things was correct. During the period 597–587/86 B.C.E. Babylon besieges, sacks, and eventually burns Jerusalem, including the Temple, to the ground, exiling its prominent citizens (Jeremiah 39; 52). The book of Lamentations, personifying Zion as a woman/mother bereaved of her husband and children, conveys the horror of this experience: "My eyes are spent with weeping; / my stomach churns; / my bile is poured out on the ground / because of the destruction of / my people, / because infants and babes faint / in the streets of the city" (Lam 2:11). Psalm 137, too, relates the anguish, but from the perspective of the exiles: "By the rivers of Babylon— / there we sat down and there / we wept / when we remembered Zion. / . . . How could we sing the LORD's song / in a foreign land?" How indeed?—but as we will see, it seems they find a way.

Exile: Exilic-Diaspora Setting (Sixth Century B.C.E.)

18. Ezekiel, Obadiah, Joel

The exile of Judeans to Babylon, beginning around 597 and culminating in the permanent diaspora or dispersion of most of the Jewish people outside the land of their ancestors, is a complex, tragic, formative, and creative period. The final chapter of 2 Kings describes soberly the Jerusalem events of siege, defeat, and the destruction of Temple, city, and civic order. The voices of Nahum, Habakkuk, Zephaniah, Jeremiah, and the plaintive voice of the Lamentations poet help draw its contours as destruction looms and is experienced in Judah, while several other characters give a sense of the actual geographical experience of life outside "the land." Among those are Ezekiel and the Psalmist. Jeremiah and Ezekiel also anticipate, each distinctively, a reversal of the exile and a return of the community, and the narrator of Kings drops a mysterious hint about survival of the last king, but we will leave the return narrative for Isaiah's "heirs" to tell.

Ezekiel, priest and prophet, is the most extensive and dramatic witness of and to the exile in Babylon. His carefully dated pieces suggest that he goes east with the first group of exiles taken in 597, including King Josiah's grandson King Jehoiachin and other members of the court. Ezekiel's ornate visions take us back in time and space to the causes of the catastrophe, as he is shown in retrospective visions certain cultic abuses tolerated and even valorized in the Temple, practices seen as so heinous and polluting that the prophet describes the solemn and ominous departure of the deity from city and Temple. Ezekiel's ministry, carried on extensively by mime, gesture, and imagery, enacts the horror of the gap grown between God's deepest desires and the behavior of the nation. It is easy to imagine how his enigmatic and wordless preaching might first have intrigued and then likely offended those attending to his communications as his indictments emerge into some clarity. His silent enactment of the experience of exile, of siege, and of death seeks to show the exiles the nature of their experience, perhaps to ritualize it in liturgy. Ezekiel's oracles and denunciations, cast into strong and bitter language, fill out the detail of his understanding of the causes of the sinfulness that lands the leadership of the Judean community in their Babylonian situation of exile. Ezekiel's violent visions explain and his parables instruct the exiles, and the homeland community as well, as to their predicament and options.

The more prosaic life of Babylon's new immigrants is less clear. Jeremiah's letter to them (Jeremiah 29) suggests that the group enjoys a fair degree of autonomy, is able at least to settle, build, plant, marry, and reproduce without too much overt oppression—and yet the composer-singer of Psalm 137 brings forth, if succinctly, the sadness and anger of the exiles, cut off as they feel from their traditions, unwilling to recite and perform their songs and stories for their captors. A matching sentiment is discernible in the short prophecy of Obadiah, who excoriates Judah's neighbor Edom for abetting Babylon's destruction and for exulting over Judah's ravaged condition. Ezekiel concludes his communication with an elaborate vision of a Jerusalem Temple rebuilt (Ezekiel 40–48). It is a sketch of a worship site wholly purified from former lapses, constructed with idealized proportions and characteristics, almost forbidding in its tidy design and clear boundaries. Ezekiel's rich if bizarre imagery offers just one indication of the vitality that comes to sustain the Babylonian community. The decades between the arrival of the first exiles and the accession of Persian Cyrus to the Babylonian throne are largely hidden in the biblical narrative, implied primarily in the community's activity of converting the centuries of lived experience into the durable language that survives in the biblical tradition to this day.

19. (Second) Isaiah of the Return

His voice emerging at the opposite end of the Babylonian exile from Ezekiel's, a figure somehow adding (or added) to the Isaiah scroll and thus sharing the name of his forebear, this prophet announces to his people a fresh opportunity to return to Judah (Isaiah 40–55). Naming Cyrus of Persia as an anointed servant (or messiah) of YHWH, "Second Isaiah" (as some call him) raises his voice to proclaim liberation, announcing and describing not only a new exodus through the wilderness but even a fresh creation. He seems to preach primarily to the exiles themselves: to some who are eager to return and also to others who resist the opportunity. But a well-trained ear can also pick out the prophet's enunciations to or for the community of those whose experience post-collapse is in Judah rather than in Babylon. These citizens are envisioned, if not directly addressed, by the prophet, their sense of welcome for returning exiles pictured as well as a sentiment less eager to greet and absorb returnees. Isaiah's subtle language hints at a realistic situation: As we will see, the return from Babylon, though celebrated in poetry and theology, turns out to be difficult; the home community, having missed the dominant and eventually dominating experience of those in Babylon and their consequent appropriation of it into tradition, will find it difficult to receive the returnees—in fact, to be welcome in their midst.

Besides his words about return, Isaiah speaks of God in fresh and cosmic imagery, as if putting to rest any sense that YHWH has been defeated by the heavenly host of Babylon. God is described as crafting the heavens and earth like a master architect and builder, as maintaining the vast stretches of Mesopotamian land and water like a skilled engineer. The prophet contrasts such a deity with the feeble and fragile lumps of wood and hunks of rock worshiped locally (in Babylon, and perhaps elsewhere too), lampooning the religious practices of the Babylonians and their ilk in extravagant and parodic terms. Though you may suspect that some of the exaggeration is more whistling in the dark than conviction about how their foreign hosts actually worshiped, there is no doubt that Isaiah is scornful in the extreme of any cult that does not recognize YHWH's majesty and transcendence, the divine holiness and power.

Isaiah is perhaps best known for his depiction of the servant of the community, perhaps an individual leader (some think he is describing himself) or possibly the community itself (the motifs are dispersed throughout chs. 42–53). Like Ezekiel's, though in a wholly different register, Isaiah's preaching helps his people to anticipate, recognize, and grow into its new status as God's servant: attentive to the divine word, non-entitled to privilege, making its way ever closer to the divine presence. The mysterious servant figure prospers, thanks to my presence as God's spirit, but not without suffering. There is misunderstanding and rejection, stemming most likely from within the exilic community itself rather than from more obvious Babylonian opponents. The servant is persecuted, rejected, punished, and yet somehow survives and thrives. The profound prophetic poetry of the servant figure, whether drawing on the prophet's own experience or that of the group, makes helpfully visible the vocation of YHWH's people as they make their own, and yours as well, the intense experiences of the sixth century. One way to think about the prophet's eloquence is as response to the poetry in Lamentations and to God's silence therein.

20. Tobit, Daniel, Esther

Three other (sets of) stories are set in the exilic-diaspora time-space, helping you open up at least in your imaginations some of the ways in which the community of away-from-the-homeland Jews would have lived. I say "imaginatively" to remind you that the stories set in exile are not necessarily meaning to reflect exact details of actual life, sometimes pretty apparently to the contrary!

The story of Tobit, set actually in the earlier exile of the northern kingdom within the Assyrian empire, depicts a pious man, Tobit, who perseveres in living Torah even in inconvenient and dangerous times. Tobit is willing to assist the poor and bury the dead even when such works are proscribed. But his resolute piety does not offset an apparent chance event of blindness, caused by something that falls into his eyes as he sleeps outside, head uncovered, on a warm night. Like Job, Tobit's patience is strained, and he lashes out at others, notably his wife Anna, who chastises him in return. Tobit finally sends his son Tobias to collect a debt owed by their kin Raguel and Edna, who live some distance away. Tobias, unknown to him, is accompanied and guided on this journey, thanks to God's providence, by the angel Raphael (whom he knows as a young man named Azariah). When Tobias and his friend arrive at their destination they find that troubles have beset that family as well. Sarah, daughter of Raguel and Edna, has been the victim of an evil demon (Asmodeus), who has slain seven of her husbands on their marriage night. Discouraged, and denigrated even by her own servants, Sarah is about to give up and end her life. Her prayer rises to God, as had that of Tobit in the previous part of the story. When Tobias proposes marriage the offer is at once accepted, even though Raguel's sense of matters is made clear when he furtively digs another grave. But Tobias and Sarah, instructed to spend their wedding night in prayer, survive, and the demon is thwarted. On their return home with the needed resources Raphael also produces a special salve that restores eyesight to Tobit. Thus once again fidelity to God and God's anonymous care for the Jewish people (my specialty!) are shown fruitful. The characters praise God and live happily ever after.

The stories found in the book of Daniel (chs. 1–6) are set in both Babylonian and Persian times (so in the seventh to fourth centuries; Daniel seems to age slowly!). He and a group of other young Jews are brought to the Babylonian court to be reeducated in the ways of their captors. A series of episodes takes place, in all of which the young people have to decide how to cope with their positions of comparative privilege: Will they choose to capitulate to the demands of their captors or remain faithful to the values of their upbringing? And how will they manage to survive if they resist the lures and demands of their oppressor hosts? When challenged to eat from the royal table, to worship a great statue, or to cease praying to their own deity, Daniel and friends resist such pressure, even when dire punishments threaten: fiery furnace, lions' den. The stories show the exiles protected by God, to whom they are faithful, and the combination of God's care and the Jews' fidelity is compelling even for the foreign kings. Daniel is also able to read and interpret dreams, resembling his ancestor Joseph in this capacity. When various Babylonian and Persian monarchs have visions they cannot cope with, Daniel both correctly and boldly tells them what lies ahead, which is rarely good news for the dreamer. Daniel also has visions as well as interpreting those of others (again like the patriarch Joseph). These scenes (four of them in chs. 7–12) narrate in code events to take place on the world stage in years to come. Daniel sees giant statues and horrible beasts, all composed and described in such a way as to suggest the succession of world empires plaguing the neighborhood, which includes Judea/Yehud. So though the elements composing the scenes are not labeled precisely it seems clear enough, especially in retrospect, that the empires of Mesopotamia (Babylon, Media, Persia) and Macedon (Alexander's achievement and its successor states), and even Rome are depicted symbolically in Daniel's visions. The deeds presaged are so dreadful that an angel has to help a fearful and discouraged Daniel to understand, and part of the vision that consoles him is the assistance for God's beloved by an angel—Gabriel—or a mysterious "son of man" figure who will champion God's just against the unjust (Daniel 7). Daniel comes to learn that events are determined from the throne room of

God, earthly machinations notwithstanding. What God wills and decrees will come about eventually, though not without terrible suffering at the time of trial. These visions are sealed up by Daniel and preserved for a time when they will be needed. I will tell you later when you should review these mysterious visions again!

Another exile/diaspora story takes place when a young Jewish woman, Esther, becomes queen of Persia, chosen from all others by King Xerxes, who does not realize that she is a Jew. When an evil and powerful court minister, Haman, determines to eliminate the Jews from the whole empire, Esther's cousin and (former) guardian, Mordecai, though not admitted to her presence, sends a message that she must use her position to protect her people. Esther, recognizing that she may well endanger herself and her position if she speaks up for her people, nonetheless decides that she must try to intervene for them, even if she perishes. Planning a trap that will appeal specifically to the ego and blindspot of her opponent Haman, Esther manages to convince her none-too-bright and easily manipulated husband that Haman's desires must not be carried out. In fact, the king allows the Jews to do to their opponents the very murderous deeds that Haman had decreed in the king's name for the Jews, thus seeding one of the cycle-of-violence stories between Jews and Gentiles that seem to continue to this day. Haman dies on the gibbet he has constructed for Mordecai, and Esther and Mordecai plan the wider punishment of their enemies in Persia.

All these stories of life in the Diaspora reflect, in their own ways, on the challenges of remaining faithful to God and community under challenging circumstances not necessarily foreseen in the earlier biblical tradition.

Post-Exilic Early Second Temple Persian Judah: Persian Period (Sixth–Fourth Centuries B.C.E.)

21. Haggai and Zechariah

When the exiles return "home" from exile in Babylon beginning around 530 (those who choose to do so), they are confronted with the task of reforming and reconfiguring a society that has been deeply traumatized by the experiences recorded in the books of Jeremiah and Lamentations (granted, those occurred some decades back). And to make matters worse, those returnees are not welcomed with open arms by all of their fellow citizens who had not been exiled. In fact, the returnees must seem rather pompous and pushy with their vision of how the community should move forward. And so, naturally, the returning group meet with resistance from those who have been struggling to move ahead in their own way during the absence of their "Babylonian" sisters and brothers. What is profoundly important to note is that even without the Temple, the cult, and the land, the people of YHWH—both those in exile and those at home—manage to retain the core of their religious identity during the years in exile. In fact, they may all have become even more dedicated to YHWH as the one true god, though each community in a slightly different way.

After the anguished language of Jeremiah, Lamentations, and Psalm 137 you might assume that the chance to return home would solve everyone's problems. In fact, when King Cyrus of Persia (who has by 530 or so defeated the Babylonians) decrees the return of the exiles (see Ezra 1 for a rendering of Cyrus' proclamation), the problems just begin. Many, even most of the Judahites in Babylon are not excited by the prospect of leaving a thriving metropolis or at least a place that has become home (remember that by this time a couple of generations have been born in Babylon and only know of Jerusalem through the stories and songs their parents have recited and sung), to return to a struggling husk of a land. The biblical text you are reading indicates that a number of prophets at the time consider their task as twofold: to encourage the people that God's favor has been restored, and that at their return to Judah they would find a land newly blessed (Second Isaiah, for example), or to bolster the spirits and spark the imagination of those already resettled in (or who never left) the land. Not so easy, you should think!

The minor prophets Haggai and Zechariah seem to fall into the latter category. They can be dated to the early postexilic period, about 520 B.C.E., which is surely a very difficult time of transition for everyone. Gone is much of the abrasive rhetoric we heard in the earlier prophets. Judah has met its fate and survived its punishment, so these prophets have the more enviable task of prophesying hope and restoration: "Thus says the LORD of hosts: My cities shall again overflow with prosperity; the LORD will again comfort Zion and again choose Jerusalem" (Zech 1:17). Insofar as their rhetoric is negative at all, that animus is focused mostly against Judah's enemies: "This shall be the plague with which the LORD will strike all the peoples that wage war against Jerusalem . . ." (Zech 14:12). Still, there is an unambiguous undercurrent of caution; the people need to turn back to God, and they are called to act justly and obediently (see Zechariah 7–8, 11). Haggai has a very clear notion of what will prompt YHWH to restore favor: The people must rebuild the House of YHWH (the Temple). Cyrus of Persia has given not only permission but resources to accomplish that project (which suits his imperial purposes nicely; see Ezra 6), but some of the people, we can detect from the somewhat querulous tone of prophetic preaching, are resistant to the idea. You will not be much off base to suppose that the people who return from Babylon insist on controlling this temple enterprise, planning to staff the Temple with priests from exilic families only (with "correct" genealogies). The folks who have remained in the land are quite understandably less than enthusiastic about the community reconstruction project being carried forward on those terms. Haggai sounds like a marketing agent hired by the returnees, so enthusiastic and persuasive is his commitment to the rebuilding project! "Is it a time for you yourselves to live in your panelled houses, while this house lies in ruins?" (Hag 1:4). And to give Haggai his due, surely he sees a temple as a source of great pride and respect for these ravished people. Haggai's main theme is simple: Build the Temple, and enjoy the rewards YHWH will shower (quite literally, since rain is one of the blessings promised) on you and the land.

Zechariah's message is more complicated. This is in part because, as we have seen in the case of the pre-exilic prophet Isaiah, another later prophet writes under the same name, perhaps on the same scroll. So consider that chapters 1–8 are the work of "First" Zechariah and chapters 9–14 were added a bit later (dates are greatly debated). Still, the main themes are not hard to pick out, and sound similar to Haggai's: There are good (albeit not idyllic!) times ahead, Jerusalem's enemies will be punished, and the Temple will be rebuilt. Zechariah's message, relayed through visions and oracles, is more cosmically grand than is Haggai's. Zechariah envisions a rebuilt Jerusalem, with all the nations of the world flowing to the gates of the Temple to bow down before YHWH (Zechariah 8). This quasi-universalistic tone is a rather common and curious feature of late- and post-exilic literature (see also Second and Third Isaiah), and greatly influences later Judaism, even subsequently Christianity and Islam. Zechariah also envisions a renewed Davidic leadership, with the addition of a high priest to rule by the Davidide's side. These two together (who are identified in both Haggai and Ezra as royal Zerubbabel and priestly Joshua) represent an ideal of political and religious renewal (Zechariah 3, 4, 6) that will see the glory of Israel returned. It appears this dream never came to fruition. Zerubbabel and Joshua disappear from later literature, and Judah never really regains even the flawed independence it knew before the exile. But the longing that has given birth to it never dies and will blossom into a messianic expectation that takes many forms in later Judaism.

22. Ezra and Nehemiah

The books (also sometimes called memoirs) of Ezra and Nehemiah offer narrative accounts of this same period of return from Babylon. Ezra and Nehemiah tell the story of the return (taking the narrative farther in time as well), but these accounts are fuller and less impressionistic than the short oracles of Haggai or the enigmatic visions of Zechariah. Ezra and Nehemiah also show the Pesian perspective more fully and make prominent the new role for priestly leadership. Cyrus, a Mede who had conquered Persia and defeated Babylon, in an astute political maneuver promulgates an edict that allows for the return home of all the peoples Babylon had exiled (a fairly accurate version of this edict can be found in Ezra 1). This grant was surely designed to win the hearts and minds of his new "subjects," and if Second Isaiah's designation of Cyrus as "messiah" is any indication, Cyrus is more or less successful with the Judahites, at least.

The book of Ezra lists in great detail the members of families who return (Ezra 2; another list appears in Nehemiah 7). What you will want to consider is not so much how factual this list is, but rather what you can infer from the stress on lineage and bloodlines now in postexilic Judah. Apparently, those who can demonstrate their lineage back to the preexilic "aristocratic" families consider themselves superior to those who stay in the land or had been transferred there during Babylonian hegemony (sometimes called "the people of the land"). Nehemiah seems to make fairly explicit reference to this discord when he reports the complaints brought by the people of the land about their treatment at the hands of the nobles (Nehemiah 5). Or it may simply be that the conflict between the groups comes from vast discrepancy in experience: Those who had lived in Babylon will have had one way of life, those who struggled on in Judah quite another. You can understand that these groups will differ in their aspirations.

In any case it is especially important that only those who can demonstrate priestly descent serve in any cultic capacity (Ezra 2). Ezra is one of those priests, an expert in *torah* sent by the Persian administration in a later wave of immigration (Ezra 7–8) to promulgate and teach the law of YHWH (Nehemiah 8). Many scholars assume that the Torah/Pentateuch is codified at this time. Lacking documentation, the people of the land are considered unfit for cultic service and thus unfit for fraternization. In this aspect the story of the exiles' return to the land mirrors the story told in Joshua of the Israelites' arrival in the land and the warnings they receive about not mixing with the Canaanites and others who are already inhabiting the land. An explicit connection of this sort is made by Ezra himself when he learns that many of the returnees have married foreign women (called "daughters of the people of the land"). He rends his clothes and mourns that these Judahites have disregarded the word of the LORD given in Deuteronomy and Joshua, forbidding them to intermarry or else risk losing the land (e.g., see Joshua 24). After years of dispossession, the recollection of this warning would not be taken lightly. It is a good reminder that, although we have in this narrative been concentrating on the storyline itself (what has been happening with the characters), another crucial aspect of biblical study includes the circumstances of composition and use and the reception of these stories. But in fact the "guilty" Judahites repent and agree to expel their wives as well as the children born to them (Ezra 10)—an appalling action from your point of view, I know, but consistent with the community's prevailing concern over issues of fidelity and cultic fitness for being YHWH's people. From the perspective of Ezra and Nehemiah the return to the land represents an extraordinary act of grace and mercy on the part of God, not the less for being coupled with a decree of an imperial power. These two leaders struggle to meet the expectations and demands of both divine and human overlords.

An equally important issue in the story of the exiles' return is the rebuilding of the Temple. Cyrus's words indicate both permission and support for this project, but a future Persian king puts a stop to it when Judah's neighbors (forbidden themselves to work on the project) complain about it. As in Haggai and Zechariah, the names Joshua and Zerubbabel, priest and prince, are mentioned again in this connection, but little seems to come of their presence (Ezra 5). The Temple is finally finished during the reign of King Darius of Persia (Ezra 6) and the traditional festivals and sacrifices are reinstituted.

Nehemiah, a governor appointed by Persia who arrives a little later than Ezra, also does his part in reestablishing Jerusalem as a viable city. In spite of intense opposition from the non-Judahites in the area, he rebuilds the walls and gates of the city (Nehemiah 4). Walls are symbols of military and political prestige. He reestablishes, according to the *torah* of God, the tithing system, which supports the Temple as well as the priests and Levites. He ensures strict adherence to the Sabbath, and like Ezra he has to contend (quite harshly!) with those married to foreign women (Nehemiah 13).

Ezra and Nehemiah might be best considered single-minded, effective leaders of a community that is struggling to construct an identity based on a renewed covenant with YHWH. It is their challenge to balance the demands of their royal Persian sponsor with the complex and contradictory needs and desires of their communities, all struggling with commitment to God. The exclusion and violence Ezra and Nehemiah both preach and practice, unpalatable as it might seem now, was in the service of this goal.

23. Malachi, (Third) Isaiah, Joel

Isaiah must have been such an influential prophet that not merely one other prophet chooses to write in his name but at least three prophets use the reputation of Isaiah to authorize prophetic experience and language. Not very originally, the last of these continues to be known as Third Isaiah (Isaiah 56–66). Perhaps the easiest way to remember Third Isaiah's context is to note that most students of the Hebrew Scriptures tend to divide up the history during which the texts were written into three distinct periods—pre-exilic, exilic, post-exilic—and conveniently, we identify an Isaiah to be associated with each period. Third Isaiah is best seen as writing during the Persian period after many of the exiles had returned to Judah. Consequently his words are often associated with Ezra and Nehemiah, with Malachi, who is also best situated in this time period, and even with Joel, whose circumstances remain wholly enigmatic to scholars.

Because the preaching of Third Isaiah, Malachi, and Joel lacks specific referents it is notoriously difficult to ascertain precise situations in which to understand them, beyond the rather vague designation "post-exilic." Nevertheless, you will still get a good sense of what is important to them, even if you need to struggle to calculate exactly *when* it was important. Whereas Ezra and Nehemiah are quite concerned about the cultic and ethical purity of the society the returnees set up, Third Isaiah wants to fling open the doors of the Temple and invite in anyone, "pure" or otherwise, who will pledge allegiance to YHWH's laws. Even eunuchs and foreigners (normally excluded) are welcome under these terms (Isaiah 56). On the surface that seems a very different message from the one espoused by Ezra and Nehemiah, who warn against intermarriage and toss foreigners out of the Temple precincts. On the other hand, all these leaders share a serious commitment to the covenant, so they may not be so far apart as first seems.

Malachi has a more specific concern regarding fidelity: Much of his ire is directed against the priesthood who, in his view, have failed to attend properly to their temple duties. He enumerates their failings: The animals they offer are blemished, the Temple lacks the resources it needs to function, and the priests have acted as corrupt judges (priests in ancient Israel often served in juridical capacities). In short, they are breaking the covenant God made with the tribe of Levi, from which much of the priestly lineage takes its vocation, at least according to some portions of the Torah (see Deuteronomy 33). Malachi also deals with the issue of marriage, as do Ezra and Nehemiah, but he rails against divorce and shows no explicit interest in the issue of foreign wives. Or perhaps the mention of marriage functions primarily as a metaphor for the "adulterous" or unfaithful ways of the people with God (Malachi 2). According to Malachi the people, and priests in particular, are behaving all too much as did their forebears before the destruction of Jerusalem, and Malachi warns them (as did the pre-exilic prophets) that God is no more likely to remain impassive than before.

Malachi ends the prophetic section of the Bible on a largely dire note: He rumbles about the great and terrible day of YHWH that is coming, which few will be able to endure (Malachi 3). Such overtones are audible as well in the preaching of Joel, who describes invasions of destructive locusts.

While Malachi warns against improper cultic activity, Third Isaiah inveighs against relying too much on the power of cultic practice to protect: "Is such the fast that I choose . . . ? / Is not this the fast that I choose: / to loose the bonds of injustice / . . . to share your bread with the hungry . . ." (Isaiah 58). Like First Isaiah, this namesake struggles to impress upon the people that Wisdom is to be gained through justice, that at the core of God's covenant is a commitment to charity. Integrally connected with this concern is the issue of idolatry—through false worship the people neglect the covenant and what is at its core. Interjected into the middle of all this "fire and brimstone" is a section (Isaiah 60–62) so hopeful and jubilant it is reminiscent of Second Isaiah's joyful oracles of reconciliation: "Arise, shine; for your light / has come, / the glory of the LORD has risen / upon you" (Isaiah 60). Taken together, these alternating trajectories of doom and hope recapitulate Israel's entire story of unfaithfulness, punishment, and return. Isaiah's language reminds all hearers—ancient and contemporary—that fracture is never the last word in the story of the human-divine relationship. Still, the unending cycle of woe and weal grows wearisome, and Third Isaiah, Malachi, and Joel are early practitioners of a way of speaking about the future that sounds rather other-worldly, and looks to a time when reconciliation will be complete and the cycle will be broken once and for all: "For I am about to create new heavens / and a new earth; / . . . no more shall the sound of weeping / be heard in it / [Jerusalem] or the cry of distress" (Isaiah 65; see also the end of Malachi 3). Some scholars like to call a more developed version of this type of prophecy "apocalyptic," and it becomes more and more prevalent in later writings, as you will see!

24. Qoheleth (Ecclesiastes) and Job

Two books, not at the surface very similar in content but able to be discussed as a pair, are set loosely in the period of Second Temple Judaism (the common designation for Israel during the existence of the rebuilt Temple). Well, actually, they are not really set specifically at all, but I will discuss them here! Neither of them tells a story, except in the most general sort of way. What each brings forth for consideration is a deep and far-ranging reflection on the ways of God with human beings and the ways of some particular human beings with the quest for God. More akin to philosophical ruminations than some of our tradition, these two voices share with religious thinkers of various cultures close to them in space and time, but with those remote as well, some of the questions posed to the mystery of God. This is Wisdom literature, my specialty!

Qoheleth purports to be a royal scion, even Solomon himself, who consequently is posthumously attributed authorship of this work. Whosever the voice may be, it reflects upon a long and rather privileged life, relates varied experiments, and mulls over considerable experience. Qoheleth's conclusion—delivered pithily, though not unambiguously, many times in the work—is that all is "breath/wind/vapor," a chase after what cannot be gained. "Vanity of vanities," he exclaims in conclusion to one or another set of possibilities and propositions about how things work and what makes life worth living. The book ranges over many topics, small to great, e.g., the uncertainties and frustrations of inheritance. The narrative voice poses a variety of situations that might befall a man of means, for example losing all he has struggled to acquire. It investigates the proverbial wisdom of the Jewish tradition. And what Qoheleth seems to claim is that nothing is to be relied upon as certain, nothing counted upon in any definitive way. Qoheleth sounds to some readers like an atheist, though that is not his point about God. He strikes others as a cynic; and though some of his sayings can be isolated to sound like that, in fact such is not his basic stance, either. What this sage does is to question radically, even to deconstruct inchoatively, the superstructure of beliefs and assumptions that undergird the biblical culture (as you sample it within the Bible). He does not replace such bases with any other foundation, simply decides that the familiar, standard "biblical" norms are not so inevitable as many of his peers would suppose. Qoheleth's thought is in many ways slippery since he glides from one situation to another, shifting topics and modes of speech without much signaling. Though many have asserted that understanding him is also a vain quest, nonetheless it strikes me as worth a try, and I urge you to delve seriously into his writing.

The book of Job is as elusive, though for different reasons. Beloved of millennia of thinkers in a way not quite the case for Qoheleth, Job also has resisted resolution as to its meaning. The frame of the book (chs. 1–2, 42) describes a situation in which God and a superhuman adversary, the *satan*, wager about whether human—specifically Job's—virtue is or even can be disinterested. Does Job behave for gain, as accused? The adversary is given divine permission to afflict Job short of taking his life, and that is what happens to Job, who, of course, does not know why such dread things (loss of property, health, children) have befallen him. The large center of the book is taken up with the discussions among Job and his three friends (Eliphaz, Bildad, and Zophar) who are eventually joined by a fourth (Elihu); all aim to account for the suffering as experienced. Proceeding roughly in three rounds, where each of the three friends speaks in turn and Job responds to each, the exchange collectively accounts for a great variety of traditional thought about why humans suffer. Many readers find substantial differences among their thoughts, and that case can be made. What they all accept, without question, is that God is somehow the agent of Job's suffering (and implicitly of other human suffering as well). The friends reach more comfortably for bromides (all sin, all suffer) but then move on to more personal charges when Job resists them (you deserve it, you have secret sins). Job, for his part, calls their ready-to-hand theology into question and parries a good deal of what they comfortably assert. Job moves more deeply into the area of the (un)fairness of God, especially the silence of God who seems set to refuse Job an encounter. After the younger-seeming Elihu bursts into the fray and makes a number of useful points that Job either cannot hear or chooses to ignore, the climax of the book looms.

Out of the whirlwind, giving plenty of rhetorical evidence that the divine ear has listened attentively to the utterances of the five humans talking about how God is linked to suffering, the deity shifts ground. Moving confidently into the role of accuser of those who have been pinning various charges on the divine self with impunity, God questions Job about the mysteries of creation. God takes Job on a verbal tour of the deep and inaccessible places where God works carefully and patiently with things of which Job knows nothing. One whole chapter (28—granted, the identity of its speaker is not clear) reflects briefly on the strange and largely inaccessible workings of divine Wisdom, implying by nature imagery that much of God's way is opaque to creatures. God reviews aspects of divine life that are remote from human concerns and confidence, quizzing Job about various details in such a way that Job must own his ignorance. It is a verbal *tour de force* (not really an "answer" to the questions posed), a good match for the many more words slung by the humans at God in their efforts to probe something of which they know only part. It is a rough lesson for Job in many ways, though arguably preferable to silence and being ignored. And Job— if enigmatically—concedes he has been bested in some way by God, who nonetheless—and also enigmatically—affirms that Job has spoken well of God! The story ends by rewinding itself, which is to say Job is given "his stuff" back again and the adversary is on the loose to await another opening to test human insight and faith. The whole puzzle of human suffering is set for another debate, as you well know! The point is not so much to solve these problems as to reflect fruitfully on their many possibilities, and Job and Qoheleth are good company in which to indulge and exercise such rumination!

Late Second-Temple Judaism: Hellenistic Period (Second–First Centuries B.C.E.)

25. The Hasmonean "Maccabee" Family and Judith

There is a narrative gap in the biblical storyline, as though the story breaks off between the last of the voices speaking in the long period of Persian rule (late 600s to mid-300s) and the events set off when Alexander the Great sweeps across toward India from Macedon in the mid-fourth century. Though legends from other sources tell of the young Greek conqueror's appreciative visit to Jerusalem, the biblical tradition is surprisingly silent on this massive changing of the imperial guard, when the wind of the long Eastern hegemony (including Assyria, Babylon, and Persia) shifts to blow in from the west again. The storyline picks up the narrative in three ways. The first two are oblique. If you recall from the exilic period, there are dreams and visions recorded by the prophet Daniel, found primarily in the second half of the book, bound up and preserved for the time when they should be needed. That time of urgency ripens in the second century, when the Ptolemaic/Egyptian heirs of Alexander lose their one-hundred-(plus)-year grip on Palestine to the Seleucid/Syrian part of the inheritance, and matters begin to change. In some ways this is the last huge shift in our story (since the Romans' takeover from Alexander's Hellenistic heirs seems almost minor).

A wider angle of explanation here may help. From the beginning of the story of God and Israel there have always been "others" involved. In fact, one way to tell the story has been to catalogue the struggles of Israel to resist or deflect those foreign peoples of the ancient Near Eastern neighborhood. They are sometimes called Philistines, sometimes Canaanites; often they are specified as small neighbors who have some close if contested relationship with Israel: Moab, Edom, Ammon, Aramaean Syria, Phoenicia. And of course we have talked about the large empires: Egypt, Assyria, Babylon, Persia. Though the storyline has often set things up as a struggle of Israel to stay uncontaminated from these others, a careful reading of the narratives betrays various kinds of obvious and inevitable entanglements of culture. The question is never really *whether (or not)* to "mingle with the nations," but *how*. The period of Hellenism presses the question afresh, and strongly. The effort of the Syrian Seleucids to consolidate their position in the Levant around the turn from the third century into the second poses the problem crucially. It is in these circumstances, narrated in lavish (not to say excessive) detail in 1–2 Maccabees, that the community remembers to reach for and find solace in the visions of Daniel that had apparently anticipated its circumstances. And the story of Judith becomes relevant here as well.

The four Daniel visions we have already talked over, with their complex, allegorical, and baroque revelations to the prophet of days to come when empires will collide horribly in confrontation with God's just. The visions granted to Daniel (some in the new genre of apocalyptic), reviewed in times such as those of Seleucid domination, console and encourage the faithful people of God to trust that, superficial indications apparently to the contrary, God has things in hand. Earthly battles will be fought and Israelite blood be shed, but God's victory is never ultimately in doubt. The story of Judith offers its encouragement in a similar way. Like the Daniel narrative it is set in "other" circumstances, but that they are palpably unreal prompts me to locate them here. The Judith storyteller reaches into the imperial grab bag for its quasi-historical referents, placing a Babylonian king as Israel's fierce Assyrian opponent and mixing other geographical and temporal "facts" in liberally to set the stage. The story tells an episode of threat from "Assyria" and "its" great leader Nebuchadnezzar (whom you will recognize as a Babylonian!), who threatens the whole world with successful domination. And he is about to be successful, since only the small mountain town of Bethulia to the north of Judea stands between him and the city Jerusalem, host to the Temple. Defeat seems inevitable. The Judith storyteller spends nearly half of the story's space describing how the resources of the mighty overpower every possible geographical opponent, implying to the reader that Bethulia cannot possibly expect to withstand the powerful sweep. General Holofernes himself is sanguine, having learned from an Ammonite named Achior that, though God protects the faithful in covenant relation to him, Israel can scarcely expect to qualify for such assistance, given a string of infidelities reaching back into the First Temple period. Holofernes is in any case confident that no deity or people can withstand the mighty Assyria and makes preparations to accomplish his penultimate victory—even banishing Achior, who escapes to be rescued by the Bethulians, whom he tells of the plans falling quickly into place around them. The siege begins, and water supplies are cut off. The leadership of Bethulia has reached the same conclusion as Holofernes, that things are hopeless for the beleaguered Jews. Discussion of defeat abounds until the widow Judith arrives on the scene.

Challenging the elders with her vision and courage, Judith bargains with them to be given a period of five days, by the end of which she will have saved the town, with God's help. Her confidence shames them and her theology of determined resistance challenges the town leaders to give her—and God—this slim opportunity to follow through with her offer. She urges a wider confidence in God and demonstrates the virtues of a more robust self-confidence in the capacity of a small community—also of a valiant people—to save itself, for God's sake and with God's help. Reminding her people what the past instructs and the future requires, she sets to work. Bathing in the rationed and precious water, changing her attire from widow's weeds to clothing befitting the wife of a powerful man (as indeed she once was), Judith leaves Bethulia. Accompanied only by a single maid, Judith makes her way toward the camp of the enemy and is welcomed into the company of a vain, greedy, and lustful Holofernes, who expects to have his way with her, whatever that might entail. She appears agreeable to his hospitality except in the matter of food, insisting upon eating from her own stores (as Daniel and his companions had done as well). Her speech to the Assyrians is also pleasing in one way to those too arrogant to penetrate the doublespeak and glibness of her platitudes, but construed in another by those (astute readers) with ears to hear differently. She reiterates for her hosts the simplistic equation of retribution that Holofernes has come to understand from Achior, and "the Assyrians" are taken in. Laying a careful pattern of exiting the tent of the Great Man in order to pray regularly, Judith thus fashions into familiarity and non-suspicion an escape route she is sure to need. On the eve of the fifth and final day of the siege he is sure is leading to victory Holofernes outdoes himself in the provisioning and intake of refreshments, fortifying himself for what he anticipates as the conquest of the beautiful widow as well as the town. But he carelessly slips into a drunken stupor, enabling Judith, with the help of her maid, to saw off his head, roll the royal body up in the bedclothes, and leave the tent daintily with the head in her foodbasket. No one questions her departure, since those alert enough to see it assume that Judith is once again about her prayers. When she arrives back at Bethulia, exhibits her trophy and tells the story, the people of Bethulia are freshly encouraged that God will indeed help them. And so it occurs. The "Assyrians" are utterly demoralized by the loss of their general, and the battle is forsaken. The righteous Gentile Achior converts and is circumcised. Judith is praised and blessed. Bethulia shares the spoil of those who would despoil her, and the community's faith in God is reaffirmed, indeed reconstituted. Though many suitors seek Judith's hand, she—anomalous though it appears in the tradition—remains a celibate, finally distributing her property to others.

The books of 1–2 Maccabees, opaque in no way at all, now tell more directly the events when "the Greeks" threaten the Israelite/Judean way of life. Pushing off quickly from the tale of Alexander the Great, the two books (which do not proceed in closely-coordinated or chronological order but tell "the same" story somewhat polyphonally) make clear the seriousness of the threat from Alexander's Seleucid heirs. Though when they first take control from their Egyptian predecessor the Seleucids offer tax cuts and other concessions, shortly circumstances shift and privilege gives way to privation. The archfoe Antiochus IV Epiphanes abuses the Temple and enters the Holy of Holies. For any to keep Torah is proscribed under pain of death, and Jews are in fact constrained to do deeds of infidelity against their religion. Several episodes of such pressure are related: A mother and her seven sons are put to terrible deaths for their refusal to recant their ancestral commitments, and an old man is tormented and killed for his persistent fidelity to the ways of his forebears. A more cohesive opposition ignites one day in the town of Modein when a man named Mattathias, father of five sons (whose "surname" is Hasmonean, but who come to be known as Maccabees after the nickname given to the first young leader) kills a Jew who is about to commit an illicit sacrifice. This father and five sons, Judas, John, Jonathan, Eleazar, and Simon, rally resistance around the neighborhood and settle in for a long struggle to remove the Seleucids from the land of the ancestors. A high point comes fairly early in the narratives when the polluted Temple site is cleansed from defilement and rededicated to Yahwistic worship (commemorated to this day by Jewish communities in the festival of Hanukkah).

The books are filled with detail, corroborated in one way or another by various contemporary sources. But amid the many deeds related, two things become apparent. First, despite the enthusiasm of the narrator for the side of the Maccabees and orthodoxy, the situation and choices of action are more nuanced. After a string of victories seems to reduce the threat from the Greeks an element within the Jewish leadership wants to break off from further resistance and war. That the Maccabees insist on full steam ahead is clearly a position not shared by all others. Second, though the whole revolt begins when the Jews are forbidden to live the Law faithfully, by the end of the day Judas Maccabee's brothers Jonathan and Simon have egregiously arrogated to themselves priestly positions and powers that are nowhere envisioned for their tribe, tying them to civic leadership in an eventually lethal way. So it is apparent to careful readers that the choice— stay Jewish or go Greek; resist totally or be swamped—is misleading and false in many ways. Hellenism is working an inevitable impact on the Jewish community within its borders, and the question of how to live with fidelity to God is not well articulated by those in power. In fact, it is possible to discern within the pages of the books of Maccabees a diversity of legitimate opinion on that life-and-death topic of healthy survival, of viable practice taking root in various places (and not simply within the Second Temple establishment), being worked out in various ways. The Maccabees are neither the first nor the last to win the battle (they do inaugurate the first period of quasi-independence since the eighth century and enlarge the borders of the state to Davidic and Solomonic proportion) but lose the war as their flagrantly illegal practice and lifestyle collude with foreigners sailing under various flags too many to name, but including Greeks, Egyptians, and ultimately Romans who, finally tiring of disorder, add the rambunctious territory to the Roman empire around 63 B.C.E.

Intertestamental Period (The First Centuries B.C.E. and C.E.)

26. *Sophia in Wisdom of Solomon*

The most extensive and illuminating story of my workings with God, the cosmos, and its human denizens—you—is available in this book. I could say a lot, but let me limit myself to a few points. The main communication is that I, intimate of God, am determined and eager for the saving of the just—unnamed here, and to be understood as those who choose God. The narrative is set by Solomon, whom you know best as a king but who presents himself here primarily as a representative human being. He alludes a bit to his blue blood but mostly makes his case as a human being. Why he desires and needs me is spoken in the first half or so of the book: It becomes clear to him that what is at stake is survival—his, that of many human beings, and that of the Jews as a group—in fact, of all those who seek God. Solomon first talks rather abstractly about who Sophia is, how she behaves, how she may be found (as I go forth seeking and finding). But then around the middle of the book he becomes more specific.

He begins to tell the story of the Jewish-Christian ancestors—unnamed, though you will recognize Adam, Noah, Abraham (and Lot), Jacob, Joseph, noting in each case how I rescue them from danger or trouble. And then, referencing Moses several times, Solomon tells how the exodus people—again not named as to religion, race, ethnicity, or gender—are struggling amid their (also unnamed) foes (actually the references are to Egyptians, but also to Canaanites and other historical foes). Unlike the case with the early ancestors, the exodus generation have a clearer sense of how I am helping them choose for me and God over against the alternatives available. And in this section of the book Solomon takes a fair amount of time to explain what the difference is between those who choose me and those who refuse. Contrary to what you may think is unanimous, Solomon suggests that the arch-sin is not to be associated with Adam and Eve in the garden—so nothing about fruit or sex—but has to do with idolatry. He shows how this practice of mis-seeing and mis-speaking—and then of mis-worshiping and mis-living—comes about. It seems like the sort of mistake anyone could make, but as it is described, its lethal character comes through. Anyway, my role as described is to help the friends of God choose well, choose life and immortality, remembrance and fruitfulness over against certain other things. The stories of the exodus—from the exposing and rescue of Moses almost until the entry into the land—are reviewed (actually, quite heavily reinterpreted). The same events that the refusers of Wisdom like, those circumstances that they want to inflict on my friends, recoil on themselves. The odd thing is that at some moment in their suffering they see clearly enough what is at stake but are too committed to acknowledge it, or too stubborn to choose it. It is a profound struggle of life and death, and a wonderful transposition of the stories from the tradition that shows the possibilities of transformation available to those who choose to be friends of God and prophets. This is my gift to give.

27. Jesus of Nazareth

You may have heard me say a few pages back that the turn into Hellenism at the time of Alexander the Great was our last big corner to go around. So far as the imperial criterion is concerned, I stand by that comment. But of course from the viewpoint of Christians, this is *the* big shift. Let me make one other remark about such appraisals. In a certain sense it is beyond dispute that the coming of Jesus, enunciated variously both in the New Testament writings and in later theology, is the watershed for Christians. But let me simply reiterate what I hope has been clear all along: that the effort of God to be involved and in communication with humans—to be in Revelation, you might say—is the persistent and continuous character of God. As we look back at the tradition we see God's self-disclosure in Torah, many whisperings into the ears of the Jewish-Christian ancestors (like Moses and Elijah), the phenomenon of prophecy where God's heart is made manifest via the prophets to the Israelite society, and my ubiquitous participation as Wisdom—just enunciated within the ancient exodus story. All these patterns take coloration from and add depth to the figure of Jesus and his unique relatedness with God. It is to that story we now turn.

Jesus arrives on the Judean scene, not coincidentally, at the shift of eras, as his coming eventually signals a new way to count time. Within the story we are reviewing he comes when Judea and Galilee have been absorbed uneasily into the Roman territory and placed, in one way or another, under the rule of the Herod family (heir to the Maccabee dominion as well as coming from the Idumean desert area). So the Herods are insiders and outsiders, favored and resented in turn by those who have to deal with them.

Four Herods—and there are plenty of others implied around them, like Herodias—feature in the story that stretches ahead. Jesus' birth (my help is prominent!) is told in the first chapters of the gospels of Matthew and Luke, the details reminiscent of many of the Hebrew Bible stories I have been reprising. Jesus' lineage is Davidic but his apparent roots are Galilean, and the sources are all silent about the first decades of his life. All four gospels initiate his public ministry in a dramatic way: through baptism by John in the Jordan, retreat in the wilderness, manifestation of glory in Cana. Gathering a group of named disciples around him and surely accompanied by many other women and men with whom he interacts closely, Jesus teaches the ways of God as he envisages and even brings near the reign of God to the Jewish people, long familiar with that symbol but invited now to anticipate it in a fresh way.

Jesus' apparently short time of ministry (a few years at the most) is recounted with some variety by Mark, Matthew, Luke, and John, but all agree that his presence is tremendously attractive to many people, notably the poor but more generally those open to the picture of God Jesus makes visible by his language of divine intimacy and renders tangible in his deeds of healing. Concomitantly, his sense of the particular quality of God's rule, which Jesus interprets as inclusive and compassionate, and which he enacts as non-hierarchical and service-driven, alienates the Jerusalem leadership that has, for whatever mix of reasons already suggested to you, chosen to ally with the Romans (most famously Pontius Pilate) and their local (Herodian) surrogates. The split between Jesus and the priestly and scribal leadership of his own people is, in all the gospels (which, as we will see shortly, are written retrospectively and so with multiple and distinctive purposes), early, marked, and ominous. Jesus' many parables about God's life and deeds, his discussions of God's preferences on topics like worship and other daily praxis, and his clear challenges to those who seem committed to attitudes and practices Jesus holds sinful, can be seen in a couple of ways. First, and this is important to note, the disputes serve as a reminder that "first-century Judaism" is far from monolithic; Jesus is less radical by far than some others of his era (e.g., the group that separates from the Temple and settles at Qumran).

But second, the gospels have, by the time they take shape, become clear that certain choices must be ratified by those who will follow Jesus and (as we will see shortly) eventually pull away from post-Second Temple Judaism. To put that pair of points slightly differently: The story you read in the gospels, showing Jesus as a Jew in intense and heated but legitimate debate with other Jews about God's purposes, also takes place amid escalating tensions between various Jewish factions and the divide-and-conquer

Romans. You will not understand some of the choices that eventually come to pass without noting well the decades of struggle that seed various violent encounters between Roman overlords and oppressed Judeans and Galileans, that generate rebels and riots of various sorts, and that culminate in a vicious war (from 66–70 C.E. or so, and resumed from 132–135) that results in the destruction of the Temple, the seizure and renaming of the ancient city Jerusalem, the proscription of Jews from the region, and the "circling of the Jewish wagons" as dangerous commitments must be made, unmade, and re-made. One outcome of the Roman war is the split between what you now call Jews and Christians. Consider the possibility that it was not inevitable!

In any case Jesus' teaching, preaching, actions, and way of life bring him up against the authorities of Jerusalem, both local and "visiting." And after a final meal with his closest friends, where Jesus breaks bread and drinks wine and speaks of the significance of this meal in their company, he is arrested (with some inside help, I am sorry to say), tried, condemned, and crucified until dead. Throughout these events he maintains the commitments that have characterized his life, and then God, also good at commitments, raises Jesus from the dead, to the surprise and joy of his friends (and to the consternation of his enemies).

And so on goes the story! In the final four scenes ahead I will proceed less by individual named characters than by group responses (while naming some famous participants). Let me put it this way: The explosion of vitality and energy that comes to be called "Christianity" can be tracked in biblical writings in a number of ways, of which I will select four, each in itself visibly complex. The point is that the efforts of individuals and communities to respond to the invitation Jesus issues about life with God and neighbor take many, many forms and thrive in diverse and even unlikely circumstances. That the New Testament singles out a few ought only to stimulate you to envision others. Startups like these are among my favorite projects, as you will see from the sections I describe.

New Testament Period (Mid-First Century C.E.)

28. Jewish Christianity: Matthew, James, Jude

As is logical, a significant energy in the early response to the life, death, and resurrection of Jesus is the effort of his own community of Jews to accommodate his person and teaching into faithful living of Torah. Beyond cavil, virtually the whole set of people around Jesus were Jews, and within the broad diversity of first-century practice there is no reason to assume that what Jesus said and did would not fit well within the spacious

practice of the final days of Second Temple Judaism. The early chapters
1–8 of the Acts of the Apostles show, though schematically, this very thing.
The friends of Jesus continue to attend the Temple to worship and to trans-
act urgent business there: testifying about their experience of Jesus, talking
and debating with others about it—notably about how Jesus can have been
put to death. The earliest conversions are among Jews, as is the immediate
response, such as the sharing of goods (Ananias and Sapphira are a negative example of something that goes mostly well [Acts 5]). The speeches in
the first few chapters of Acts give evidence of the community—with its
various constituencies—relating recent events in terms of Jewish tradition.
Discussion is intense. Stephen, for example, a Greek-speaking (rather than
Aramaic-speaking) Jew, rehearses the whole question of God's "tenting"
with Israel and draws a conclusion that is displeasing to Temple authorities: the Temple was a mistake from the start (Acts 7). There are a number
of tangles with the Jerusalem authorities: James is put to death, Peter imprisoned (Acts 12). It is clear that the Jerusalem church suffers in a variety
of ways in the decades after the death of Jesus. The early forays out from
Jerusalem target primarily Jews, Samaritans, and proselytes: the Ethiopian
eunuch, the widow Dorcas, Barnabas, Cornelius (Acts 8; 9:36-42; 10:11-18;
11:22-30). In several stories tensions flare about how to sort out practical
issues, e.g., of "kosher" food laws and circumcision, and we see how these
are managed in a group where many will continue to observe such customs
as they have always done.

Another way to look for this same appropriation of the Jesus-
experience into Judaism is in the Gospel of Matthew. While telling the
story of Jesus, Matthew (like the other evangelists, as I will reiterate below)
is also shaping the story in terms of issues particular to his own communities. Scholars have seen well to suppose that Matthew is plausibly writing
for a group of (primarily) Jews who have every expectation of remaining
faithful to Torah, contested though that position is coming to be by the time
Matthew writes (a generation or so after the life and death of Jesus). Matthew
includes not only discrete quotations from the Hebrew sacred texts to show
the continuity between God's ways of old and the present, but he includes
skeins of verbal allusions as well, linking deeds of the past and present.
Jesus resembles Moses more clearly in Matthew than elsewhere. Matthew
shows Gentiles (e.g., the Magi in Matthew 2) being attracted to the
(nascent) Jesus-believing community, and the shaping and discourse of the
leader characters in the gospel intonates quite clearly some of the struggles
between Matthew's community (living, many suppose, in Antioch of Syria)
and the leadership of other Jewish groups. The faithless leaders are shown
to be those who suspect and resist Jesus, those who allow the vineyard

heritage to be trashed (notably by the Romans, who destroy the city in 70 C.E.) because of their greed and blindness (Jewish factionalism is a significant factor in the war). Characters like Levi (Matt 9:9-17) and some of the nameless ones healed on the Sabbath (e.g., Matt 12:9-37) provide alternative responses for the community members to appropriate. The issue for the Matthean group is not whether to abandon Judaism but how to live it more faithfully, and Jesus' preaching (ch. 5), his distinctive parables (ch. 13), his comparative parsings of behavior (chs. 6–7), his denunciations of scandalous behavior (ch. 23), all make the options stark. The Gospel of Matthew also stresses Jesus as a Wisdom figure (one of my children), whose life and deeds demonstrate well what is within.

The issues discussed in the short letters of Jude and James show similar patterns. These two epistles made it into the Bible because they are ostensibly written by Jesus' biological brothers (Mark 6:3; Matt 13:55; 1 Cor 15:7; Gal 1:19; 2:9-12; Acts 12:17; 15:13-21; Jude 1). Some scholars think they were actually written in the late first century, well after the first generation of eyewitnesses had died, and more "in the spirit" of James and Jude than actually by their hands. Either way they both reflect concerns of the nascent Jewish-Christian community much as Matthew does, and you would expect this especially for James, the leader of the early Jerusalem church. Like Matthew, the letter of James is concerned to promote ethical behavior along the lines of the Torah as I explained it to so many Jewish sages over the years, speaking less in the form of law than of proverbs (Jas 1:17-18, 22-25; 3; see Matt 5:17-48). There is in this letter (2:14–3:18) a heavy emphasis on the importance of works as a manifestation of faith, and the wise among you will notice the contrast between this emphasis and that of Paul. For James this issue seems to focus around disparities between rich and poor and how all are to be treated with impartiality in the assembly, an admonition that works to the greater benefit of the poor. The letter of Jude reflects different but significant points of contact with Jewish tradition, though not all of this is biblical. Jude is concerned to correct false teachings that promote a kind of intellectual salvation (gnosticism) and a complementary moral licentiousness, warning that God does have standards and judges harshly those who transgress them. He shares with Matthew and James a concern to hold fast to Jewish tradition in the face of hybrids of Jewish and Gentile customs developing in some early Christian circles.

29. Gentile Christianity: Mark, Luke

The story with which you are probably more familiar is the "growing pains" of the young community of Jesus believers as significant numbers of non-Jews become linked. If Matthew considers what will happen if a Jewish community is "salted" with a few Gentiles, the other way to ask the question is: What happens when the majority of a community is non-Jewish and has relatively little access to the whole tradition out of which Jesus came? Two gospels give us some sense of how that may have been. Mark, writing first, and many suppose from Rome (with its crazy emperors and egregious ways of treating "ordinary" people), gives his community a way to live in the heart of imperial power with fidelity and sustainability, at least in the short run. That Mark seems unfamiliar with the geography of Jesus' ministry, employs some Latin terms, and stops occasionally to explain a Jewish custom reinforces the notion that his community is heavily Gentile. The figure of Jesus made visible in Mark is a strongly authoritative leader who deals competently with other strongmen from various realms of power on and "below" earth (e.g., Mark 5). Mark's character Jesus talks starkly and apocalyptically in terms of a final cataclysm that is likely to come soon, thus offering adherents a model for the martyrdom that is all too likely for many. Mark's gospel shows the probable need to make difficult decisions between family and God-commitment (see Mark 3:9-21; 10:17-31); it also shows some Gentiles who do well when they come into even brief and unexpected contact with Jesus: the Gerasene demoniac (Mark 5:1-20), Bartimaeus (Mark 10:46-52), the centurion who draws guard-duty the day that Jesus is crucified (15:39). In fact, the testimony of this unnamed centurion to the quality of Jesus' death almost upstages the resurrection in terms of what is important to grasp.

Luke's gospel, probably also written primarily with Gentiles in mind, seems to emerge from a less tense and fraught and probably a more affluent community. Though its members, too, have to find ways to survive in the culture established by Roman rule, the issues are portrayed in slightly subtler terms. Jesus in Luke is in a certain way no less a threat to Roman values than is the case in Mark, but the discussion is set up differently. The origins of the child Jesus are set in the midst of the ordinary lives of six faithful Jews (Mary, Joseph, Elizabeth, Zechariah, Anna, Simeon), who though in each case startled at the new deeds stirred up by me, nonetheless adapt suitably and in ways useful to non-Jews (Luke 1–2). The figure of Jesus in Luke's recital is most notable for the many parables in which he verbally draws God, ceaselessly and lovingly at work with creatures (many cluster between chs. 9–19). The "Lukan" parables abound with imagery and insight derived from the close observation of nature and are spoken by a poet who loses no opportunity to show how what is most familiar and ready to hand is replete with the presence of God's action. But the human characters in the parables are perhaps the most salutary for those struggling to reimagine how God suffuses the lives of those longing for God's touch: not only the "good" but the "bad" characters in the parables of Pharisee and Publican, Widow and Judge (ch. 18), the prodigal father and sons (ch. 15), the various players surrounding the Good Samaritan (ch. 10), and countless other figures offer endless possibilities for insight of one kind or another and appropriation of what is needful. This is true of other gospel characters as well: Simon the Pharisee and the unnamed woman who anoints Jesus (ch. 7), Zacchaeus (ch. 19), the two thieves crucified with Jesus, even the unnamed disciples who walk with him to Emmaus. All of these help direct Luke's community well along its path.

I have already spoken of Luke's second book, the Acts of the Apostles, when I narrated the earliest growth of the church in Palestine. The second half of Acts, set somewhat schematically, traces the growth of the community beyond the borders of Palestine and beyond the tables of Jews and God-fearers, highlighting the phenomenal response of Gentiles to the good news as well as a number of issues that need to be faced as they flock into the communities. Since much of that story centers around Paul, let us shift now to what Paul can show us about the response to Jesus, both as we meet him in the Acts of the Apostles and as we examine the issues absorbing his letters to the churches.

30. Gentile Christianity: Paul, 1 and 2 Peter

I have hinted that the early Christian church should really be imagined as *a lot* of early Christian churches, just as there were several Judaisms in Jesus' day. You can see this if you read the New Testament texts closely, and particularly if you read the letters of Paul, a former Pharisee trained in Jewish law who becomes an apostle to the Gentile world. Paul is a controversial figure from day one, and the seven letters he wrote that survive in the Bible clearly reflect some of the battles he engages in—with Jews and Gentiles to be sure, but also with others committed to Jesus!

The central issue that Paul addresses is over the Jewish Law: Whereas the leaders of the Jerusalem church think that new converts to Christ have to follow it, Paul believes that faith in Christ is enough for salvation (Rom 1:17; 3:28). This central debate pits Paul against the leaders of the Jerusalem church, namely James the brother of Jesus and Peter (Gal 1:18–2:14), as well as countless Jews he crosses paths with on his journeys (Acts 14:19; 17:1-15; 18:12-17). Unlike many other Jewish Christians, Paul believes that faith in Christ offers something the Law could not give, namely justification (see all of Romans). To Paul's mind the Jewish Law only has the power to point out where one has failed; neither the Law nor careful observance of it can actually *make* one righteous. So he promotes a kind of faith focused on the power of the cross as the initial triumph of God's new creation, which Paul believes God has begun to reveal powerfully for the salvation of the world. Paul's is an apocalyptic spirituality in that he believes that God is in the midst of revealing (the root meaning of apocalypse) a renewed world, and that the final revelation or restoration is coming soon.

In addition to the debate over the ongoing relevance of my earlier revelation through the Law, there are other controversies too, such as whether Paul can even claim to be an apostle (Gal 1:1–2:10), fractures among Christian groups based on which teacher they follow (1 Cor 1:10-17), misinterpretations of Paul's advocacy of celibacy (1 Corinthians 7–11), and grace (Romans; 1 Corinthians 12; 1 Thessalonians). With all of these battles so apparent in Paul's own letters it becomes all the more striking that Luke's history of the early church in Acts presents Paul minus most of the controversy as an agent of the natural and relatively irenic expansion of Christianity into the Gentile world (compare Gal 1:18–2:14 with Acts 15)! Attentive readers do well to wonder what Luke is up to.

As you can probably already tell, the seven letters that most scholars think Paul actually wrote (or had a scribe write for him) are unparalleled sources of insight into the early Christian world. They provide a first-hand account of the personalities of the first generations of Christians and the issues that vex them. In a fascinating passage in the letter to the Galatians, in the context of a self-defense, Paul tells us of his fidelity to Judaism (Gal 1:13-14; Phil 3:4-6) and of his own conversion to Christ while on his way to persecute Christians, presenting himself in the style of the prophet Jeremiah (Gal 1:15-17; see Jer 1:4-10). This likely happens around the year 35 C.E. He recounts the event again in 2 Cor 12:1-10, but here he speaks of "a person" he knows being "caught up to the third heaven," an allusion to an ecstatic experience he had in the context of his conversion, when he encounters me more directly. Now while these stories and what I have recounted so far may indicate a man with a healthy ego, I should point out how careful Paul is to say that he is *not* eloquent (1 Cor 1:17–2:5), that he is "content with weaknesses, insults, hardships, persecutions and constraints for the sake of Christ" (2 Cor 12:10), that he, like the lord he serves, is a servant and even a slave of Christ (Philippians 1–2).

This may well be why, for all the conflicts that Paul seems to have with fellow Christians, Jews and Gentiles, he develops a correspondingly large number of colleagues and friends as well who are willing to share in the hard work and danger of building the Christian community. These characters usually appear at the beginnings and ends of his letters, where Paul thanks those who convey his missives and maintain the communities he has visited. Romans and Corinthians are especially rich in this regard, introducing us to Paul's coworkers, the married couple Prisca and Aquila, his fellow apostles Andronicus (a man) and Junia (a woman), and the whole household of Stephanas in Corinth that appears to be ministering *en masse* to the Corinthian church. The Acts of the Apostles mentions some of these individuals and adds others, such as Lydia, a wealthy woman in Philippi who appears to host the nascent community in her home (16:11-15; 18). And in both Paul and Acts we hear of his close companions like Barnabas, Timothy, Mark, and Silvanus.

One thing is certain: Paul is the hero of the late-first-century Acts, and by that time he has already had an enormous impact on the Christian church and on the shape of the New Testament. In addition to the seven epistles written by Paul, an additional six claim to be by him and are more or less written in his spirit (2 Thessalonians; Colossians; Ephesians; 1–2 Timothy; Titus), and there would be other letters in the second century written in his name (e.g., *Laodiceans* and *3 Corinthians* [both non-biblical]) or collected in groups of seven (the Epistles of Ignatius). In addition, several other late New Testament books reflect an awareness of Pauline teaching, notably 1–2 Peter, which I will mention momentarily. And then there is a host of apocryphal and entertaining stories that show the ongoing influence of Paul in the early Church, particularly among ascetic and gnostic communities (e.g., the *Acts of Paul and Thecla*). This flurry of literary activity, along with the influence of Paul on later Christian sages like Augustine and Martin Luther, have led to a belief commonly expressed that Paul rather than Jesus was the founder of Christianity—something that Paul himself would have vehemently denied (1 Cor 1:13-17; 3:5-23; Gal 2:19-20).

There are two little and late letters in the New Testament that seem to depend somewhat on Paul, namely 1–2 Peter. Both of these letters are ostensibly written by the chief disciple of Jesus according to the synoptic tradition, but scholars debate the likelihood of that attribution. Now it may seem odd, given everything I've been saying about tensions in the early church, that letters in the name of Peter would have anything in common with the letters of Paul. But such is the nature of early Christian history that as time and teaching develop, new syntheses are possible, and even actively help to weave together the various strands of the scattered community. In fact, two circumstances in particular create the new cloth: persecution from without (1 Pet 4:12–5:11) and false teaching from within (2 Peter 2). Under these pressures Christians renegotiate who is out and who is in, and so figures formerly at odds like Peter and Paul appear closer to each other than the new threats appear to the traditional teaching (e.g., compare

1 Pet 1:3-5 with Gal 4:26; Phil 3:20). It is a little less surprising that a book written in the name of Peter would depend on a work associated with Jewish Christianity like Jude, but this too is clearly the case in the admonition about false teaching (compare 2 Pet 2:1-18 with Jude 4-16). The last body of material in the New Testament, the Johannine literature, introduces another and entirely different kind of synthesis possible in the expanding Christian community.

New Testament Period (Late First Century C.E.)

31. Alternative to The Great Church: the Johannine Communities

It just goes to show that categories are hardly adequate to contain what we are talking about here. If we think in terms of primarily Jewish or primarily Gentile we falter a bit at this next swath of texts. The Johannine community—a sort of artificial construct derived from the Gospel of John, the three short letters of John, and the book of Revelation (also known as the Revelation to John or Apocalypse of John)—defies that easy polarity. What I can offer you is this: The Johannine community represents an alternative to the Great Church, that community more familiar to you from the gospels, the letters of Paul, and the Acts of the Apostles (keep in mind that only a fraction of the early experience has come down to you in the Bible). And the "Johannine community" instructs you to hold out for the most likely possibility that the origins of what comes to be called Christianity—the hugely fruitful moment when the figure of Jesus enters the culture of the Hellenistic-Roman Jewish world—is richly explosive in terms of forms of communal response.

But since we are dealing with biblical texts, John is our example for that fruitfulness: gospel, letters, apocalypse. All three suggest a time period near the end of the first century (some scholars believe they may even have been written into the 100s C.E.). And the clearest supposition, you will think, is that the community we can call Johannine is alert to Hebrew Bible (Old Testament) allusions. So we are dealing with a community substantially Jewish. But it is as clear that there has been a fundamental and painful break with Judaism, perhaps even an expulsion of some of the Johannine community from communion with the synagogue. The gospel makes clear the struggle, both in terminology—as it references "the Jews" as a negative pole and as it relentlessly positions Jesus in controversy with the leaders of the Jerusalem community. Perhaps the clearest place to watch the struggle unfold before our eyes is in the triangulated encounter between the man born blind, Jesus, and the authorities (John 9). It seems clear enough from the discourse that the blind man—and even his parents—must choose an interpretation of what has happened. The stakes are great, and the man whose sight has been restored starts carefully as he explains it, but when pressed he becomes bolder in his affirmations, until he is put out of the Temple/synagogue for what he professes. His parents are careful, and the story does not further track them or the response they represent. But their choice also is stark and painful. There has been some sort of clear break from the inside, perhaps from the outside as well. As we look at some of the vivid and memorable characters in this gospel we get a sense of the membership of the Johannine community: surely Jews (Nicodemus represents the conflictedness of the leadership element [John 3]), but also Samaritans—the woman at the well (John 4). These, as well as certain passages we might look at in Acts, help us begin to sort the complex relationship between Samaritans and Jews. There is evidence of diaspora Jewish membership as well, even of Gentile participation in the community (John 12), so we can appreciate the "multiculturalism" of these small churches and perhaps get a sense of why their testimony goes a different route from the synoptics. The community has been placed traditionally in Ephesus, but consider the possibility of Alexandria as well, the city that gave rise to Wisdom of Solomon with its vast resonances with this gospel!

For that is, perhaps, the most important thing to notice. John's gospel not only offers an alternative storyline to the events of the historical Jesus (the outline of the gospel is quite alternative to the synoptic order, the operational calendar varies, the discourse is in a substantially different register); but the whole way of talking about who Jesus is and what he does takes a wholly different track. The clearest example, perhaps, is that in Mark, Matthew, and Luke, Jesus preaches the reign of God and tells parables to both clarify its nature and bring it closer to hand. In the fourth gospel, though there is rich figurative language aplenty, there are few parables. Jesus, contrarily, talks in symbols (water, bread, light, life [in chs. 4, 6, 9, 11 respectively]) and then in long and complex discourses that ramify various points (in 4, 6, 7–8). There is minimal reference to God's reign, rather extensive rumination on God's gift of eternal life, and careful suggestion about how such a gift might be received. The other dynamic distinctive to John is the mode of leadership: Rather than the clear prominence given to Peter in Acts and the synoptic gospels, the signal presence is the shadowy beloved disciple, whose *persona* (somewhat merged with the writer of the gospel—called John in tradition) becomes ever clearer as being the access to Jesus and the rich community with the Father, the Spirit, and other believers that is available. Before leaving the discussion of this gospel let me go back and mention some of the superb characters we meet there: the mother of Jesus, Nicodemus, the Samaritan woman at the well, the man born blind, the family of Mary, Martha, and Lazarus, the Beloved Disciple, and Mary of Magdala.

The letters of John, which I will connect here, are short pieces written by an elder—clearly in a position of authority—to communities (churches) who know him but from whom he is absent, at least at the moment. He refers vaguely, it may seem, to certain situations involving how the members of the fellowship will talk about Jesus in relation to God. It seems that, by the time of the writing, some expressions are acceptable and some are not. There is division broadly hinted—a clear "us" and "them," and in fact the need to talk about (again in somewhat veiled language) how some of them used to be us but are no longer with us. The rifts among friends are clear, the dissension and rivalry, and ultimately the going forth or expulsion are clear. The letters struggle with certain issues, notably hospitality, that pertain after certain lines have been drawn clearly: Whom to receive and whom to reject are issues of great moment if not of total clarity to "outsiders" reading much later.

The third of the "Johannine trilogy" is the book of Revelation. An apocalypse somewhat like the second half of the book of Daniel, the narrative tells of certain visions or revelations made to one John, a resident of Patmos, who seals them up but then makes them known at the proper time. Like Daniel's visions, those revealed or unveiled to John tell of the workings of God in the end times, how the triumph of God over various enemies will be accomplished. Like Daniel's revelations, John's are filled with rich symbolism from the Hebrew Bible and with imagery from cult and worship, presumably from "current events" as well (whether from the war events of the 66–70 tangle between Judaism and Rome, from Temple liturgy, from natural disasters, or from the genre of imagining the end of the world). They are addressed to a set of communities in Asia Minor, instructing them as to the right conduct of their lives as Christians living amid the violence of the Roman empire. Whether those communities are experiencing full-fledged persecution (not so likely) or simply harassment and fear—dreadful enough—the main point of the instruction is that they persevere in fidelity to what they have been taught and know, dire circumstances notwithstanding. As events in the great struggle between the forces of good and those of evil escalate, the beloved communities need to know how to survive, and their assurance that God has foreseen and foretold—and controls—all events, including the fall of the dread Babylon (also known as Rome) are part of the reassurance. Though the language of the final Revelation—and the new Creation that unfolds from it—seems in some ways far removed from most of the other ways in which God's presence with humans (and with the whole cosmos) has been pictured, the narrative elements from the tradition are the common alphabet holding it in place.

The story of the Scriptures I inspired over so many years ends here for Christians, and it ends where it began: at the moment of Creation. Although the book of Revelation presents its creation as entirely new—a new, temple-less Jerusalem descended from the sky with Christ reigning forever—the vision of the future is really a vision brought forth from the past, of a kind of paradise from which all evil has been purged. In this way the Christian Bible closes as the Hebrew Bible does in 2 Chronicles, with a vision of a restored Jerusalem serving as symbol of God's enduring love for God's people. It has been enjoyable for me to tell you of these wonderful biblical characters, to deepen in your minds and hearts these great events that are foundational to your lives. More could be said, and will be, in the volumes of the INTERFACES series. These scenes are simply a reference point, a reminder of the large outlines of the story. Read carefully but read creatively! The experience of the ancestors, the carefully prepared and preserved narratives and texts, and especially the divine care that supports and enlivens your existence just as it cared for the people of God will continue to assist. Call upon me for wisdom as you proceed! You may sense me present to you, helping you find new insight from these ancient and well-loved stories.